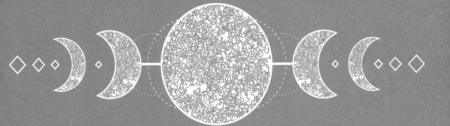

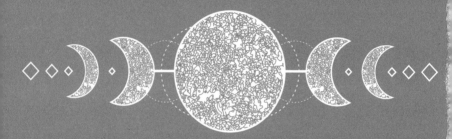

Moonology
Diary 2021

Yasmin Boland

HAY HOUSE

Carlsbad, California • New York City
London • Sydney • New Delhi

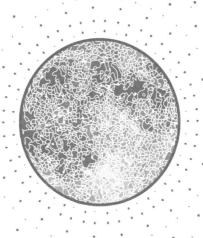

This diary belongs to

···

Published in the United Kingdom by:
Hay House UK Ltd, The Sixth Floor, Watson House,
54 Baker Street, London W1U 7BU
Tel: +44 (0)20 3927 7290; Fax: +44 (0)20 3927 7291
www.hayhouse.co.uk

Published in the United States of America by:
Hay House Inc., PO Box 5100, Carlsbad, CA 92018-5100
Tel: (1) 760 431 7695 or (800) 654 5126
Fax: (1) 760 431 6948 or (800) 650 5115
www.hayhouse.com

Published in Australia by:
Hay House Australia Pty Ltd, 18/36 Ralph St, Alexandria NSW 2015
Tel: (61) 2 9669 4299; Fax: (61) 2 9669 4144
www.hayhouse.com.au

Published in India by:
Hay House Publishers India, Muskaan Complex, Plot No.3, B-2,
Vasant Kunj, New Delhi 110 070
Tel: (91) 11 4176 1620; Fax: (91) 11 4176 1630
www.hayhouse.co.in

Text © Yasmin Boland, 2020

The moral rights of the author have been asserted.

All rights reserved. No part of this book may be reproduced by any
mechanical, photographic or electronic process, or in the form of a
phonographic recording; nor may it be stored in a retrieval system,
transmitted or otherwise be copied for public or private use, other
than for 'fair use' as brief quotations embodied in articles and reviews,
without prior written permission of the publisher.

The information given in this book should not be treated as a
substitute for professional medical advice; always consult a medical
practitioner. Any use of information in this book is at the reader's
discretion and risk. Neither the author nor the publisher can be held
responsible for any loss, claim or damage arising out of the use, or
misuse, of the suggestions made, the failure to take medical advice or
for any material on third-party websites.

A catalogue record for this book is available from the British Library.

ISBN: 978-1-78817-364-3

Interior images: 23: 123RF and Shutterstock; all other images
WumiStudio/Creative Market

Printed and bound in Italy by Graphicom

Contents

Welcome to 2021!

Let's get straight to the point: 2020 was a big year, and 2021 is going to be massive too, as some of the most intense astrology we've seen for a while is coming our way. This will be a year in which important life changes are *practically inevitable*. Therefore, it makes sense for us to *work with* the year's big energies: to use them to consciously create our life as much as possible. So, what do *you* want to create for yourself and what do you want to change about your life?

This Moonology diary considers the crucial influence that the *overall* planetary energy will have on our lives in 2021, while focusing on the high points of the *lunar energy*. It zooms in on the year's New and Full Moons, and the lunar eclipses, which herald – and sometimes even seem to force – the changes we need to make. We'll also track the Moon's phases, and take into account the Supermoons and the single Blue Moon of 2021.

Note that the information and practices in this diary are as transformational as they are simple, but you have to *do* the work required. I've received stunning feedback from people who've successfully tapped into the lunar cycle while using a Moonology diary. The Moon and stars are *free and accessible to everyone*, and the Moon especially is *amazing* for manifesting, so if you've dabbled in manifesting with mixed results, using the Moon as a cosmic timer could be the missing magical ingredient you've been searching for.

Lunar Overview 2021

So, what can you expect from the planetary and lunar energies in 2021? As you go into the year, it's a time to live consciously and intentionally. Be conscious of where in your life you feel good, versus where you feel trapped. Also look at where you could be making someone else feel trapped! Be intentional about breaking free. Look at the lessons life's teaching you. Face up to the truths that will liberate you.

The good news is that the 2021 energies are also *motivating*, so we should all feel inclined to do whatever we can to live our best lives. Sometimes there'll be sheer frustration as you try to make changes and it all feels stuck. But keep going, staying conscious and mindful. Liberation awaits you on the other side of the hard work.

The planetary alignment that will influence us strongly this year is a clash between Saturn and Uranus that occurs every 20 or so years. Uranus is the planet of change and revolution, of breaking free and awakening. The less you resist the changes that 2021 is pointing you towards, the easier, better and more exciting the year can be. Saturn is the planet of hard work and karma. He's demanding the best of you in 2021, as he always does, so make your aim true.

Plus, there are plenty of make-something-happen angles between the planets, so we're all being given a motivational kick in 2021. This may show up as the shock of truth setting us free, experience showing us the ties that are binding, breaking through old structures or busting through fear.

Happily, lucky and confident Jupiter will also be involved, at least at the start of the year. In January, Jupiter makes a big clash (everything Jupiter does is big) with chaotic Uranus. Hopefully this will bring us all a wonderful wake-up call that sets us up for the rest of the year. Jupiter is clashing here, but, in the words of Robert Hand (arguably the most respected astrologer in the world), 'There's no such thing as a bad Jupiter transit.'

The main thing to keep in mind as we go into 2021 is that everything happens for a reason. Whether you find this easy or hard to accept will depend on your life experiences. Regardless, it's definitely food for thought this year.

Let the Moon Be Your Guide

As you move through the intense astrology of 2021, keep coming back to the Moon with the help of this diary. As you connect with the New and Full Moons, you'll feel their energies swirling. Think of the Moon's beautiful and gentle rhythm as a kind of song that helps you to tune in to the cosmos and keep time as the days pass.

No matter where you are in your life right now, it's my hope that you'll use the Moon to get yourself to a better place by the time 2021 is over. What it is you're scared of or boldly hoping for, allow this diary to guide you towards achieving your goals and manifesting your dreams. It *can* happen!

So, join me on this journey into 2021 with the Moon as our guide.

Understanding the Lunar Cycle

The introduction to this diary is just the start of the conversation we're going to have over the next 12 months about working with the magical lunar cycle. In this section we'll explore the main 'phases' of the Moon, and how best to use their energies, but first, here's a tiny bit of mystical Moon history, in no particular order.

Interest in the Moon has been growing these past few years – have you noticed? I strongly believe this is related to the re-emergence of the Divine Feminine, which started at the end of the 20th century with the Harmonic Concordance (Google it!) and the famous 1999 total eclipse of the Sun.

One by one, women are taking back their power, and a key part of that is harnessing the energies of the lunar cycle. Women have been working with the Moon for millennia and human–Moon history stretches even further back – cave markings in France reveal that the New and Full Moon were being noted as early as 25,000 years ago.

I believe that the Moon is ingrained in our psyche from infancy – surely every mother everywhere holds her baby in her arms and points up to the sky with a bright 'look at the Moon!' I know my mother did this with me and I did it with my son.

The Moon's Eight Main Phases

In 1967, famed US astrologer Dane Rudhyar published a seminal book called *The Lunation Cycle*, in which he divided the motions of the Moon into eight main phases. Nearly everyone since who works with the Moon astrologically has based their ideas on his, including me. What follows is a Rudhyar-inspired explanation of the Moon's phases, put through my own filters of research and experience.

Note that a lunar cycle lasts *around* 28 days and covers the time it takes for the Moon to complete one revolution around the Earth and to move through all 12 zodiac signs.

The New Moon

The New Moon is amazing. It's all about new beginnings, and it's when we make New Moon wishes (we'll look at these later). Essentially, New Moon is the start of the new lunar cycle, and for our purposes, it's a time to settle down for a good 20 minutes or so to think about life plans. It's the start of the waxing cycle, when the Sun and the Moon are on the same degree of the zodiac at the same time.

The Crescent Moon

This is the next phase, occurring from 3½ to 7 days after New Moon. It's when we get the sliver of the New Moon up in the sky. Energetically, it's the time to really go for it, in terms of manifesting whatever we want to attract into our life. As you'll see shortly, making New Moon wishes doesn't stop when you blow out the candle and stop listening to Deva Premal.

◑ *The First Quarter Moon*

This phase occurs from 7 to 10½ days after New Moon. It's when the Moon, which was in the same place as the Sun around a week ago, makes a 90-degree angle to the Sun as it moves forwards in the skies. At this point we're halfway between New Moon and Full Moon. Rudhyar warned that crises can arise at this time – all the better to test how committed we are to our New Moon wishes: do they have legs; do we believe they have legs; do we have to work harder to manifest them?

◐ *The Gibbous Moon*

This Moon phase comes 10½ to 15 days after New Moon. I sum it up by saying that this is when we start to *feel* all our feelings. Gibbous means 'bulging' and if this Moon frequency holds our emotions, which I believe it does, it's when our emotions are likely to feel as if they're bulging out of our emotional pants!

○ *The Full Moon*

This phase occurs from 15 to 18½ days after New Moon, when the Sun and Moon are exactly opposite each other. It's the climax of the lunar cycle: the emotional explosion. This is the time when people start to act out because they're feeling all their feelings. Surrender is also a key concept now – Full Moon is when we surrender our wishes to the Divine.

This is my favourite part of the cycle as I'm much more comfortable with a big round Moon that I can see. I also feel it's at Full Moon that wishes live or disappear – we surrender them to the Divine and see what happens.

◗ The Disseminating Moon

This phase occurs from $3\frac{1}{2}$ to 7 days after Full Moon. It's when we disseminate it all – when we breathe out, and share what we've learned as we go into the far more yin waning cycle, which lasts until New Moon. Breathe, and let it go.

◑ The Third Quarter Moon

This phase occurs from 7 to $10\frac{1}{2}$ days after Full Moon. It's a quiet time in which we just keep processing. Crises can come up again. What are you learning? What's life showing you? For me, it's a time to meditate more, to intuit my way. Remember, too, that as author Mike Dooley says, thoughts become things, so choose the good ones as you move through this darker part of the cycle.

◕ The Balsamic Moon

This phase begins roughly $10\frac{1}{2}$ days after Full Moon and continues to the beginning of New Moon. It's the dark time when we need to retreat. Balsamic means healing – use this time for healing and soothing, because next we'll go back into the brightness of the waxing cycle, to be birthed by the mysterious, invisible New Moon.

Working with the Moon's phases with the help of this diary will change your life in ways you can't imagine! You'll draw on the Divine wisdom of the feminine, brought to us through the ages, against tremendous odds.

Working with the Astrological Houses

In this diary, you'll find a super-simple way of discovering where in *your* personal astrological chart the monthly New and Full Moons are taking place and how to use that information to make predictions for yourself.

In the New Moon and Full Moon sections of each month is a heading called 'What this lunation means for you', under which is a list of the 12 Star signs alongside a numbered 'House'. Before we go any further, let's look at what a 'House' is in astrology. Note, too, that there's an explainer video about this on my site (moonmessages.com/diary2021).

An Overview of the Houses

Every month the New and Full Moon affect, or 'trigger', a part of your chart that astrologers call a House. There are 12 Houses and each relates to a specific area of life: for example, there's the 7th House, which is your Love Zone; the 10th House, which is your Career Zone; and the 12th House, which is the deepest and darkest part of your chart. Here's a brief summary of what's governed by each House.

The 1st House: your appearance and image; self-identity; how you come across to others.

The 2nd House: cash, property and possessions, and values – including how you value yourself.

The 3rd House: communication; siblings; neighbours; quick trips; early learning and education.

The 4th House: home and family; all things domestic; where you belong; your past.

The 5th House: romance; creativity; kids (your own or someone else's); pursuit of pleasure; love affairs.

The 6th House: daily routines, including at work; your health; duty.

The 7th House: your lovers, your spouse and your ex; open enemies; any sort of partner, including business partners; cooperation and competition.

The 8th House: joint finances; credit cards; debts; sex; anything you consider taboo; inheritance; transformation.

The 9th House: study; travel; the Great Cosmic Quest; the Internet; higher learning; religion; spirituality; dreams.

The 10th House: your career and ambitions; how you make your mark on the world: your reputation.

The 11th House: friends; networks; social circles; hopes and wishes.

The 12th House: the deepest, darkest, most sensitive part of your chart. Your fears; your spirituality; self-undoing; withdrawal; secret or hidden enemies.

Making Predictions at New and Full Moon

When you come to the 'What this lunation means for you' headings each month, find your Star sign/numbered House combination in the list and then return to *this section* to read the information for that House in the guides below; this will give you a forecast for your month ahead.

However, for a super-accurate forecast, it's best to read it for your Rising sign. This is the most personal point in your chart because it's based on your time, date and place of birth. If you don't know your Rising sign you can calculate your chart for free at my site (moonmessages.com/freechart).

The New Moon through the Houses

The 1st House

The New Moon is taking place in your 1st House this month, which is big news. It offers you the chance to start again in any part of your life in which you know that's needed. If you're really happy with the way things are going then consider an energy recharge to help propel you through the coming 12 months. If you want to change the way others see you, the next four weeks are the time to work on that.

The 2nd House

A New Moon in your 2nd House is all about cash, property and possessions. If you want changes in any of these aspects of your life, this New Moon is the ideal time to start to make them. Money is energy and it responds quite quickly to our thoughts of abundance. If you've been thinking negatively about money, use this New Moon as a marker and decide to turn around your thoughts and expectations about it.

The 3rd House

When it comes to getting what we want, it's great to visualize and write wish lists, but also to communicate to others what we want. This invokes the law of attraction because speaking our desires means we need to have some conviction that we can get what we want. The New Moon this month in your Communication Zone brings energy galore for communication. What do you want? Who can help you? Just ask.

The 4th House

Your home life, your personal life, your domestic life, your past, your family, the people who feel like family and your actual home – all these parts of your life are up for renewal now as this month's New Moon focuses its energy onto your 4th House. If you haven't been getting on well at home or with your family, this is the ideal time to sort things out. If you want to move, sell or buy, it's all possible.

The 5th House

Welcome to the House of Fun! Have you been having a bit of that lately? If not, then the skies are strongly suggesting that it's time to get out and do a little bit of what you fancy. Could you use a restart in terms of romance, creativity or kids? Identify which one(s) you want to work on and draw up an action plan. What could you do to inch closer to what you want? Remember, the law of attraction means we can't get what we want until we know what we want.

The 6th House

In one way, this is a dull and tedious House because it's the part of your chart that's all about your daily routines – not exactly riveting. However, this is also the part of your chart where you get a chance to tweak your schedules and routines so that, at the very least, your daily life runs in a way that pleases you. If minor changes are needed in these areas, this is a great month to put them in place.

The 7th House

How's your love life? There's a New Moon in your Love Zone this month, which means you're getting the chance to reinvigorate your love life. If you're single, this is the perfect time to move on from old loves, old dreams and any old heartaches. If you're attached, you're probably aware of the importance of keeping your relationship fresh – and this New Moon brings in fresh energy and a chance to think about some of the things you and your partner can do this month.

The 8th House

You have the New Moon in your 8th House this month. That means it's firing up the part of your chart that deals with sex and money. If your love life is dull, do whatever it takes to rev things up. If you've been inhibited, try something new. Go as far as you feel comfortable. Moneywise, it's all about where your money is involved with someone else, so you have a chance for a restart in terms of your income or salary; plus, it's a very good time to set up a debt repayment plan.

The 9th House

This part of your chart is related to study, travel and adventure. There's a rush of new energy in these areas of your life, so if you have plans for them, ask for the skies' support. This part of your chart is about seeing The Big Picture of your life. It's about higher learning and self-improvement. This is the month to open your eyes to the big wide world, rather than fretting about all the little details on the home front.

The 10th House

This month's New Moon is flooding your professional or student life with potential and ambition. If you're already on the right path in your working life, then this lunation can really amp things up. However, if you're struggling professionally and not quite sure where to turn, use this New Moon as a marker. Over the coming four weeks, really put yourself out there – research your job market and talk to experts who can help you get where you want to be.

The 11th House

The New Moon in your 11th House relates to your friends and the things you're wishing for. Having the New Moon here is very auspicious for two reasons: firstly, it means that, over the coming four weeks, you're in a cycle when you can meet new people, so be open to having new friends in your life; secondly, it's a hugely important time for manifesting.

The 12th House

You're in a slightly strange cycle – can you feel it? This month, the New Moon is taking place in the part of your chart where you keep All Matters Hidden and Spiritual. This can be a time when you just want to withdraw from the world, or, if you're on a spiritual path, you might want to take time out from the madness to meditate. Know that the Universe will deliver the messages you need to hear.

The Full Moon through the Houses

The 1st House

It's all very well being focused on someone else, but once a year the Full Moon reminds you that you also need to focus on yourself: and that time is now. Many of us are givers rather than takers, and this can mess with the flow in our lives. So, this month remember to say *yes* when people offer help. You could feel emotional during this cycle, but a lot of the 'stuff' that's coming up *needs* to be dealt with!

The 2nd House

Balance is required between what you do for yourself financially and what you do for others. Consider your income and your debts; your self-worth and what others pay you, which is usually based on what you ask for. If you're about to make a major purchase, you're doing it at the right time. If you've been letting someone control you because they have financial power over you, this is your chance to break free.

The 3rd House

It's all very well dreaming of the Great Escape to a far-flung corner of the world or even the nearby countryside, but what about the details? This Full Moon is reminding you that things need to be taken care of close to home. It's also a reminder to express yourself. If you haven't been honest about how you feel, now is the time to start to say your piece. Dramas with siblings can be sorted now too.

The 4th House

Working like a dog to achieve your personal goals seems like a good thing, but there's a time and a place for everything. Right now, you're entering a cycle when you need to find a balance between your outer aims and your inner needs. Take a look at your family relationships and ascertain whether everything is running as smoothly as you'd like. If not, this is the time to pour some energy into that part of your life.

The 5th House

The Full Moon is taking place in your House of Self-Expression so there's a whole lot of emotion going on now. For some, it's all about pouring your heart out; for others, it's about the joy a child brings or pouring emotion into a creative project. And between all this, you need to find a balance between your Self and your friends. Don't neglect them totally! This is your challenge for the coming month.

The 6th House

If you're one of the lucky ones, this is the Full Moon when you see yourself for who you *really* are – your good points and your flaws – and you decide to do something about your flaws. This is all about the daily life you lead. Are you living healthily, exercising, and getting enough sleep? If not, then this Full Moon is your annual chance to start taking care of yourself – body, mind and spirit.

The 7th House

This Full Moon suggests it's time for you to step aside a little and invest some emotional energy in other people: your significant other, business partner or even an adversary. At the very least there needs to be a balance – it seems someone else needs your attention. The Full Moon can also bring closures, so if you're in a friendship or relationship that's ending, you can proceed in the knowledge that you're finishing things up at the right time, celestially speaking.

The 8th House

This Full Moon is all about finding a balance between give and take. If you know you've been doing too much of either, it's time to redress the balance. When you give too much but don't know how to take, how can the Universe send you an abundant stream of good things if you're not receiving them without a fight? Now is a good time to attend to practical financial matters, like paying off debts. It's also very good for investing some emotion in the boudoir.

The 9th House

Personal growth, religion, philosophy, publishing, the Internet, travel, and study – these are just some of the subjects looming large for you now as the Full Moon takes place in your 9th House. Be honest with yourself: have you been fussing too much over the details of your latest problems or tasks? If so, step back and look at the big picture of where you are and where you want to be. This is a great time to try something that's beyond your usual everyday realm.

The 10th House

If you've been hiding yourself away and generally keeping a low profile, watch out. The skies are suggesting loudly that it's time for you to step out of the shadows and back into the limelight. As tempting as it might be to slouch around at home, this Full Moon in your 10th House of Career is telling you it's time to invest some emotional energy in your professional life. If a work situation is coming to an end, something new will come in its place soon enough.

The 11th House

Of course, it's tempting for everyone to focus on our own pleasures. Life is for living and having fun after all. However, this month's Full Moon in your 11th House is reminding you that you need to find a balance between indulging yourself and remembering that the people in your life also need some attention – from you. Whatever you do now for someone else, you'll get extra karmic brownie points. This also makes the coming month good for networking.

The 12th House

Life has probably felt very busy recently and no one can blame you for wanting to take some time out. The Full Moon in your 12th House is going to allow you to do just that. For many people, it comes at a time when they're feeling a bit down; however, you're probably just exhausted from the demands of daily life. Take some time out. If you know how to meditate or practise yoga, go for it. You need to strike a balance between working and time out.

How to Use This Diary

If this is the first time you've used a Moonology diary, let's take a look at its main features.

Full Moon Forgiveness

Full Moon is the best time to practise forgiveness and gratitude, and to release negativity. It's a yang time. So on each month's Full Moon we do a forgiveness ceremony by writing a 'forgiveness list' and then burning it. Write your Full Moon forgiveness list on the diary page provided, but if you can't bear to tear out and burn the diary page itself, transfer your list to a piece of paper and burn that instead.

Full Moon forgiveness is our monthly emotional clear-out, opening up our channels for better manifesting. You can do your forgiveness ceremonies with me (for free) every month on Facebook (see moonmessages.com/fbevents), with friends or alone – *they will change your life*!

New Moon Wishing

Next comes the New Moon, which is when we make wishes for ourselves, our loved ones and for the highest good of all. It's a very yin time. New Moon is when we effectively 'sow the seeds' of our dreams by writing down our wishes and intentions. Each New Moon, you'll find a diary page to create your 'wishes and intentions list'.

When you're doing this, try to avoid just dashing it down and thinking 'that's done' before racing off to the next thing. Remember: you get back what you put out. Always listen to the creative visualization meditation I've created for you at moonmessages.com/diary2021 before doing your wishing 'work'. Then turn your #1 wish into an affirmation by writing it down as if it's *already real*, then *feeling* it as real as you say it out loud with gusto and passion. *That's* how you make your wishes come true.

Conscious Creation

I really hope that you'll complete the forgiveness and wishes and intentions lists at every Full and New Moon, along with the 'Questions to Ask at This Full/New Moon' pages. These practices *really* work, but you have to do them. Sometimes they will apply more than others – which is fine.

When you do your forgiveness ceremony, all this goes double. Making wishes brings amazing clarity – and it can feel like the main event when you're consciously creating – but in fact, if you're all bunged up with resentment, upset and other negative feelings, your wishes won't go out into the world clearly. It's the monthly Full Moon forgiveness we do that helps us to banish the self-doubt that could otherwise block our manifesting. Crucially, forgiving yourself will help you to release. You're worthy of your greatest dreams. You'll understand more about this as you work through the diary.

Noting the 12 Signs of the Zodiac

It's a good idea to keep your diary close to you, because each day it tells you which zodiac sign the Moon is in; see the chart below for the glyph, or symbol, for each sign. Make a note of how you feel under particular signs.

Aries	♈	Libra	♎
Taurus	♉	Scorpio	♏
Gemini	♊	Sagittarius	♐
Cancer	♋	Capricorn	♑
Leo	♌	Aquarius	♒
Virgo	♍	Pisces	♓

The Moon moves very quickly through the zodiac – going through all 12 signs every month. What you might not know is that as She goes, the Moon triggers other planets: for example, harmonizing with Venus or clashing with Pluto.

It's hugely edifying to work out where the Moon is in relation to your Star sign on any given day. In a nutshell, if the Moon is in a Fire sign (Aries, Leo or Sagittarius) or an Air sign (Gemini, Libra or Aquarius), that bodes well for Fire and Air sign people. Whereas if the Moon is in an Earth sign (Taurus, Virgo or Capricorn) or a Water sign (Cancer, Scorpio or Pisces), it bodes well for Earth and Water sign people.

All this said, my biggest tip for using this diary is to take a moment to say or write down what it is you're grateful for: calling in or releasing... every day.

Have a wonderful 2021!

What I'm Drawing into My Life in 2021

Make a list below of everything you want to attract into you life in 2021. It's a super-powerful thing to do.

_____

_____

_____

_____

_____

_____

_____

_____

_____

_____

_____

_____

_____

_____

My 2021 Action Plan

For each of the things you want to attract into your life, list at least one *action* you can take towards making it happen.

_____

_____

_____

_____

_____

_____

_____

_____

_____

_____

_____

_____

_____

Weekly
Diary

JANUARY

M	T	W	T	F	S	S
				1	2	3
4	5	6	7	8	9	10
11	12	13	14	15	16	17
18	19	20	21	22	23	24
25	26	27	28	29	30	31

FEBRUARY

M	T	W	T	F	S	S
1	2	3	4	5	6	7
8	9	10	11	12	13	14
15	16	17	18	19	20	21
22	23	24	25	26	27	28

MARCH

M	T	W	T	F	S	S
1	2	3	4	5	6	7
8	9	10	11	12	13	14
15	16	17	18	19	20	21
22	23	24	25	26	27	28
29	30	31				

APRIL

M	T	W	T	F	S	S
			1	2	3	4
5	6	7	8	9	10	11
12	13	14	15	16	17	18
19	20	21	22	23	24	25
26	27	28	29	30		

MAY

M	T	W	T	F	S	S
					1	2
3	4	5	6	7	8	9
10	11	12	13	14	15	16
17	18	19	20	21	22	23
24	25	26	27	28	29	30
31						

JUNE

M	T	W	T	F	S	S
	1	2	3	4	5	6
7	8	9	10	11	12	13
14	15	16	17	18	19	20
21	22	23	24	25	26	27
28	29	30				

JULY

M	T	W	T	F	S	S
			1	2	3	4
5	6	7	8	9	10	11
12	13	14	15	16	17	18
19	20	21	22	23	24	25
26	27	28	29	30	31	

AUGUST

M	T	W	T	F	S	S
						1
2	3	4	5	6	7	8
9	10	11	12	13	14	15
16	17	18	19	20	21	22
23	24	25	26	27	28	29
30	31					

SEPTEMBER

M	T	W	T	F	S	S
		1	2	3	4	5
6	7	8	9	10	11	12
13	14	15	16	17	18	19
20	21	22	23	24	25	26
27	28	29	30			

OCTOBER

M	T	W	T	F	S	S
				1	2	3
4	5	6	7	8	9	10
11	12	13	14	15	16	17
18	19	20	21	22	23	24
25	26	27	28	29	30	31

NOVEMBER

M	T	W	T	F	S	S
1	2	3	4	5	6	7
8	9	10	11	12	13	14
15	16	17	18	19	20	21
22	23	24	25	26	27	28
29	30					

DECEMBER

M	T	W	T	F	S	S
		1	2	3	4	5
6	7	8	9	10	11	12
13	14	15	16	17	18	19
20	21	22	23	24	25	26
27	28	29	30	31		

DECEMBER 2020 WEEK 52

....

21 MONDAY

Winter Solstice/Yule (northern hemisphere) and
Summer Solstice/Litha (southern hemisphere)
....

22 TUESDAY

....

23 WEDNESDAY

....

24 THURSDAY

....

WEEK 52   DECEMBER 2020

○ ♉   FRIDAY 25

○ ♉♊   SATURDAY 26

○ ♊   SUNDAY 27

THIS WEEK

*This week brings a planetary alignment known as
The Great Conjunction: Saturn and Jupiter are meeting for
the first time since 2000. Harness the energy by being both
optimistic and realistic about your goals for 2021.*

January

The start of 2021 has a message: 'Don't get too comfortable, because the wheel's still in spin!' As the new year dawns, we're all still feeling the eclipses of November and December 2020, and the very recent moves of mighty planets Jupiter and Saturn into Aquarius – they haven't been in that sign together like this since 1405.

We sense that life's changing, even if we're not quite sure how. Be grateful if you're feeling excited – you should be, because it's a big year ahead. Moreover, there's a Jupiter/Uranus clash on 17 January, and that's a big shake-up/wake-up call waiting to happen. It can either be super-jarring, or used to our advantage.

If you want to slough off 2020, *now* is the time to do it. But you have to be living consciously and intentionally. Connecting with your Higher Self and the Divine through meditation, chanting and prayer will help. This is the time to draw an energetic line under the past.

The Jupiter/Uranus clash this month promises that we can make changes. This year isn't one to be started complacently. Rather, look at January as a chance for big change. Where do you already know this needs to happen? Perhaps your New Year's resolutions take this into account –

and if not, perhaps they should. Change is super-supported and needed this month, but with Fixed signs (aka those that love to maintain the status quo: Taurus, Leo, Scorpio and Aquarius) predominating, it might not always be easy. Regardless, decide what needs to change now.

M	T	W	T	F	S	S
				1	2	3
4	5	6 ◑	7	8	9	10
11	12	13 ●	14	15	16	17
18	19	20 ◐	21	22	23	24
25	26	27	28 ○	29	30	31

~ Things to do this month ~

1. Wake up to something you've been trying to avoid.
2. Make some massive changes in your life.
3. Make a new start professionally.

DECEMBER WEEK 1

....

28 MONDAY   ♊︎◯

....

29 TUESDAY   ♊︎♋︎◯
Full Moon
Los Angeles   19:28
New York   22:28

....

30 WEDNESDAY   ♋︎◯
Full Moon
London   03:28
Sydney   14:28

....

31 THURSDAY   ♋︎♌︎◯

....

Week 1 January

○ ♌   Friday 1

○ ♌   Saturday 2

○ ♌ ♍   Sunday 3

This Week

Happy New Year! This week brings the last Full Moon of 2020, in the sign of Cancer. Life could be a tad confusing now. Happily, by New Year's Day, most of us should be feeling more centred and inspired.

JANUARY WEEK 2

....

4 MONDAY   ♍ ◑

....

5 TUESDAY   ♍♎ ◑

....

6 WEDNESDAY   ♎ ◑

What are you grateful for right now?
....

7 THURSDAY   ♎♏ ◑

....

☽ ♏

FRIDAY 8

☽ ♏ ♐

SATURDAY 9

☽ ♐

SUNDAY 10

THIS WEEK

We're now in the waning cycle of the Moon, so it's the time to release whatever you have left over from 2020 that you know has to go. Write it all down in a list, and then burn it.

New Moon in Capricorn

The key energies of this Moon are:
Hard-working • Solid • Realistic • Explosive

Place	Date	Time	Degrees
London	13 January	05:00	23:13
Sydney	13 January	16:00	23:13
Los Angeles	12 January	21:00	23:13
New York	13 January	00:00	23:13

'Explosive' isn't a word you'd necessarily associate with Capricorn. However, this Capricorn New Moon is super-charged as it's taking place near the planet of explosions and fireworks, transformation, passion and power: Pluto. So, expect this first New Moon of 2021 to pack a punch – and treat it with respect. This really is a New Moon to work with. In fact, all New Moons are great to work with, but this one is (a) coming at the start of the year, when resolutions are high, and (b) near the life-changing planet Pluto.

Take a moment to think about this. If your life were to be transformed by the end of 2021, what would it look like? What would you have released from your life, and what would you have kept? Where in your life do you want to reinvent yourself? Where do you want to be professionally by the end of 2021? This New Moon can help you with that. Keep these ideas in mind as you fill out your New Moon wishes and intentions list over the page.

There's a rather tough Mars/Saturn clash happening just after the New Moon, too. So there could be issues arising around wanting to move forwards and being held back by fear, rules, an authority figure or something else. If you're feeling that, make your plans anyway. The intentions you set will outlast this planetary clash.

The good news is that before too long, the tensions will be replaced with energies that will smooth dramas and ruffled feathers. Be sure to listen to the New Moon creative visualization meditation at moonmessages.com/diary2021 before you do your wishing 'work'!

⋇ What This Lunation Means for You

To discover where the energy of this New Moon is for you, find your Star sign or Rising sign here, see which House is involved, and then read the New Moon through the Houses guide (*see pages 10–14*): Aries – 10th House; Taurus – 9th House; Gemini – 8th House; Cancer – 7th House; Leo – 6th House; Virgo – 5th House; Libra – 4th House; Scorpio – 3rd House; Sagittarius – 2nd House; Capricorn – 1st House; Aquarius – 12th House; Pisces – 11th House.

● Your New Moon Affirmation ●

My life is transforming and I'm reinventing myself.

New Moon Wishes and Intentions

It's vital to get 'in the zone' before setting New Moon intentions and making wishes. Each month, visit moonmessages.com/diary2021 and listen to the meditation for the New Moon. Then write your list with an open heart – feeling excited about what you're creating. *Feel* the feeling of a wish fulfilled, and think about taking inspired action to make it real.

_____

_____

_____

_____

_____

_____

_____

_____

_____

_____

_____

_____

_____

Questions to Ask at This New Moon

What am I scared of?

_____

_____

_____

_____

How does that fear hold me back?

_____

_____

_____

_____

What transformation do I want to see in my life in 2021?

_____

_____

_____

_____

_____

JANUARY WEEK 3

....

11 MONDAY ♐ ♑ 🌑

....

12 TUESDAY ♑ 🌑

New Moon
Los Angeles   21:00

....

13 WEDNESDAY ♑ ♒ 🌑

New Moon
London   05:00
Sydney   16:00
New York   00:00

....

14 THURSDAY ♒ 🌑

....

● ♒ ♓   FRIDAY 15

◑ ♓   SATURDAY 16

◑ ♓   SUNDAY 17

THIS WEEK

The New Moon is banging up against Pluto and a Mars/Saturn clash.
If someone is cramping your style, or making you sad, see if you can get
away from them… without them noticing! Healing crises are possible.

JANUARY WEEK 4

18 MONDAY ♓♈

19 TUESDAY ♈ ◐

20 WEDNESDAY ♈♉ ◐

What are you grateful for right now?

21 THURSDAY ♉ ◐

☽ ♉   FRIDAY 22

☽ ♉♊   SATURDAY 23

☽ ♊   SUNDAY 24

This Week

*Watch out for electricity on 20 January as Mars, the fiery
planet that loves to pick a fight, meets Uranus, planet of
electricity, under the Crescent Moon. Try not to blow a gasket.
Be nice, and be kind to yourself and others. Breathe!*

Full Moon in Leo

The key energies of this Moon are:
Flashy • Confident • Healing • Challenging

Place	Date	Time	Degrees
London	28 January	19:16	09:05
Sydney	29 January	06:16	09:05
Los Angeles	28 January	11:16	09:05
New York	28 January	14:16	09:05

When you consider the energies of this Full Moon, they seem contradictory: how can they be both healing *and* challenging? Well, it's like life. Both astrology and Moonology can resemble a box of chocolates with lots of flavours, and this week, there are quite a few different energies in the skies.

For one thing, the Full Moon is in Leo, which is all about showing off what your mama gave you. Parade about, sure, but also balance your need for centre stage with the needs of those around you. Upping the ante is that at the time of this Full Moon, the Sun is on top of (so to speak) ebullient Jupiter. In fact, the Sun and Jupiter are on the very same degree of the zodiac as the Full Moon takes place –

what astrologers call *partile*. Jupiter amplifies, so the fun of the Leo Full Moon and the need to find a balance are exacerbated. Every Full Moon is emotional, but this one is likely to be even more so.

This Full Moon has healing notes too, because committed Saturn and the healing planetoid Chiron are harmonizing. So, where does 'challenging' come into it? For one thing, it'll be a challenge to stay cool and calm under this fiery Full Moon alongside Jupiter. For another, caught in the crosshairs of the Full Moon we have Mars, the planet of anger and determination, who always revs things up.

What This Lunation Means for You

To discover where the energy of this Full Moon is for you, find your Star sign or Rising sign here, see which House is involved, and then read the Full Moon through the Houses guide (*see pages 14–17*): Aries – 5th House; Taurus – 4th House; Gemini – 3rd House; Cancer – 2nd House; Leo – 1st House; Virgo – 12th House; Libra – 11th House; Scorpio – 10th House; Sagittarius – 9th House; Capricorn – 8th House; Aquarius – 7th House; Pisces – 6th House.

Release 2020

This could be a rather intense Full Moon – all the better to feel all your feelings under it. It's the first Full Moon of the year, too, and therefore the ideal time to get into a clear headspace. The Full Moon is the perfect time to let go and move on. So, what do you need to *release* from 2020?

Full Moon Forgiveness List

Make a list of who and what you're forgiving and releasing from the past and then burn it. Forgiving doesn't mean what happened was okay – just that you're letting it go. It also releases karma. Be sure to forgive yourself, for whatever you think you did, or failed to do. Come on: give yourself a break. Do better next time.

_____

_____

_____

_____

_____

_____

_____

_____

_____

_____

_____

_____

_____

Questions to Ask at This Full Moon

Have I scuppered myself by letting my ego go crazy? And if so, what can I do about it?

_____

_____

_____

_____

Am I willing to take a deep breath before arguing? If not, why not?

_____

_____

_____

_____

What are some of the ways I can create my own luck?

_____

_____

_____

_____

JANUARY Week 5

....

25 MONDAY   ♊ ♋ ◯

....

26 TUESDAY   ♋ ◯

....

27 WEDNESDAY   ♋ ◯

....

28 THURSDAY   ♋ ♌ ◯

Full Moon
London   19:16
Los Angeles   11:16
New York   14:16

....

FRIDAY 29

Full Moon
Sydney   06:16

SATURDAY 30

Mercury goes retrograde (until 21 February).

SUNDAY 31

THIS WEEK

*Mercury, the planet of communication, is going retrograde
in Aquarius this week. This is a great time for intellectual
growth. You can throw out any outmoded ideas based on
what you think is right and replace them with facts.*

February

This month kicks off with love and abundance planet Venus moving into Aquarius on 1 February and then connecting with serious Saturn. This 'flavours' the start of what's effectively 'Valentine's month'. It's good news if you want to make a deal, or even get married (which is a sort of deal, or a contract, at least).

Saturn is about business, the long term, commitments and contracts. It's good if you want to get more serious in love. However, it could also make the start of this month feel as if there's not enough love to go around. So, if you find yourself feeling like that, turn it around by doing something very Venus (abundance)/Saturn (strategies), such as making yourself a 12-month financial plan, or even seeing a business advisor.

Valentine's Day could be a bit up and down for some, and not necessarily in a good way. Speaking frankly (we're all adults here, right?) Valentine's sex could be amazing, and it'll be easier to talk about your feelings; however, hot on the heels of this is a Saturn/Uranus clash. So go easy on yourself and your partner if it all feels a bit tense. The last thing you should do if you're in a partnership of any kind is try too hard to control matters, because that could backfire. At the same time, if someone is trying to force you to do things their way, there's a very good chance you'll rebel.

Also this month, Mercury retrograde ends on 21 February. In other words, anything you do between 1 and 21 February will be done under Mercury retrograde, and for that reason it could end up being *redone*.

M	T	W	T	F	S	S
1	2	3	4	5	6	7
8	9	10	11	12	13	14
15	16	17	18	19	20	21
22	23	24	25	26	27	28

— Things to do this month —

1. Let it go, let it go!
2. Learn the lessons that life is teaching you.
3. Get back on track.

FEBRUARY WEEK 6

1 MONDAY   ♍︎♎︎ ☽

Festivals of Imbolc (northern hemisphere) and Lammas (southern hemisphere)

2 TUESDAY   ♎︎ ☽

3 WEDNESDAY   ♎︎♏︎ ☽

4 THURSDAY   ♏︎ ☽

What are you grateful for right now?

☽ ♏︎↗ ♐︎   FRIDAY 5

☽ ♐︎   SATURDAY 6

☽ ♐︎♑︎   SUNDAY 7

THIS WEEK

There's a lot of Venus (love and abundance) action this week. Your best bet is to be serious and open to radical turnarounds. Avoid trying to fence anyone in (especially ahead of Valentine's Day).

New Moon in Aquarius

The key energies of this Moon are:
Feisty • Detached • Optimistic • Electric

Place	Date	Time	Degrees
London	11 February	19:05	23:16
Sydney	12 February	06:05	23:16
Los Angeles	11 February	11:05	23:16
New York	11 February	14:05	23:16

This New Moon looks interesting – but it has its limitations. Flavouring it is a meeting between communicative Mercury and loving Venus. So if you want to make a new start when it comes to love or the flow of abundance into your life, get clear now.

This is also the time to declare your intentions regarding your love life and your finances – to someone else and/or to the Universe – and to turn your #1 New Moon wish into an affirmation (*see page 19*). However, there are other big energies to bear in mind. Wait at least 13 hours after the New Moon, because immediately following it, the Moon is Void of Course (meaning that it doesn't make an aspect with any planet until it moves into the next sign of the zodiac), and it's said that whatever you start then won't bear fruit. This is the only time the Moon goes Void of Course straight after the New Moon in 2021.

Not long after the New Moon but before the Full Moon, we get the Saturn/Uranus clash, so there'll be something of a 'crack it wide open' energy around. Ask yourself: 'Am I *resisting* a lesson that I need to learn – and if I just take it on board, will I be liberated from someone or something?' That's the question of the month.

Be sure that if an authority figure is giving you instructions that are rubbing you up the wrong way, you're not just being hard to get along with. On the upside, this energy is amazing if you want to tear down old structures in your life, literally or figuratively.

This New Moon also heralds the Chinese New Year: the Year of the Metal Ox.

☆ What This Lunation Means for You

To discover where the energy of this New Moon is for you, find your Star sign or Rising sign here, see which House is involved, and then read the New Moon through the Houses guide (*see pages 10–14*): Aries – 11th House; Taurus – 10th House; Gemini – 9th House; Cancer – 8th House; Leo – 7th House; Virgo – 6th House; Libra – 5th House; Scorpio – 4th House; Sagittarius – 3rd House; Capricorn – 2nd House; Aquarius – 1st House; Pisces – 12th House.

● Your New Moon Affirmation ●

Love and abundance now flow into my life.

New Moon Wishes and Intentions List

Make at least one wish related to where the New Moon is taking place for you (see 'What this lunation means for you'), and also make a wish for world peace – if you can spare it. Imagine the power that would be generated by people all over the world wishing as one for world peace... I know, right?

_____

_____

_____

_____

_____

_____

_____

_____

_____

_____

_____

_____

Questions to Ask at This New Moon

Have I been detached to the point of appearing uncaring? With whom and why?

_____

_____

_____

_____

Do I actually believe in my own abundance? And if not, how can I change that?

_____

_____

_____

_____

Which structures in my life do I need to smash down and break free from?

_____

_____

_____

_____

FEBRUARY WEEK 7

8 MONDAY ♑ ◑

9 TUESDAY ♑ ◑

10 WEDNESDAY ♑ ♒ ◑

11 THURSDAY ♒ ●

New Moon
London   19:05
Los Angeles 11:05
New York   14:05

Week 7 February

♒♓   FRIDAY 12

New Moon
Sydney   06:05

♓   SATURDAY 13

♓♈   SUNDAY 14

THIS WEEK

There could be some relationship challenges this New Moon/
Chinese New Year/Valentine's Week, but it really is a case of least
said, soonest mended. Valentine's night looks potentially romantic,
but there are unsettled energies in the air… so go easy!

FEBRUARY WEEK 8

15 MONDAY ♈ ◐

16 TUESDAY ♈ ◐

17 WEDNESDAY ♈♉ ◐

18 THURSDAY ♉ ◐

FRIDAY 19

What are you grateful for right now?

SATURDAY 20

SUNDAY 21

Mercury retrograde ends.

THIS WEEK

*Mercury ends its retrograde in the sign of Aquarius this week.
Whatever you've been putting off doing because Mercury was
retrograde, you can start to think about implementing.*

Full Moon in Virgo

The key energies of this Moon are:
Freedom • Positive thinking • Culmination • Order

Place	Date	Time	Degrees
London	27 February	08:17	08:57
Sydney	27 February	19:17	08:57
Los Angeles	27 February	00:17	08:57
New York	27 February	03:17	08:57

It's time to find a balance between dreams and reality; between fantasies and what it's actually going to take to get your life in order. This is the challenge of the Virgo Full Moon, which takes place when the Sun is in poetic Pisces and the Moon is in organized Virgo. This creates a tug-of-war between the side of you that wants to stare at the stars all night and dream your way through the day, and the part that knows the i's must be dotted and the t's crossed.

Finding a balance between these two parts of ourselves is important. Tap into the positive energies and harness the Mercury/Jupiter link that's taking place around the same time as the Full Moon. Mercury is about communication and Jupiter is about looking on the bright side.

Make a list of what you want to make space for in your life and then do your Full Moon practices – they are designed to help you let go of whatever's blocking you. We practise forgiveness because it releases karma and lightens our load.

✳ What This Lunation Means for You

To discover where the energy of this Full Moon is for you, find your Star sign or Rising sign here, see which House is involved, and then read the Full Moon through the Houses guide (*see pages 14–17*): Aries – 6th House; Taurus – 5th House; Gemini – 4th House; Cancer – 3rd House; Leo – 2nd House; Virgo – 1st House; Libra – 12th House; Scorpio – 11th House; Sagittarius – 10th House; Capricorn – 9th House; Aquarius – 8th House; Pisces – 7th House.

✳ Forgiveness and Karma Release Formula

This formula is based on the work of Catherine Ponder and is used with her kind permission. On the night of the Full Moon, read it out loud, or silently:

Under the glorious Full Moon, I forgive everything, everyone, every experience, every memory of the past or present that needs forgiveness. I forgive positively everyone. I also forgive myself for past mistakes. The Universe is love, and I'm forgiven and governed by love alone. Love is now adjusting my life. Realizing this, I abide in peace. I bring love and healing to my life. I've learned my lessons. I call on my soul fragments to be cleansed and to rejoin me. I send love to myself and everyone else. I'm healed. My life is healed. And so be it.

Full Moon Forgiveness List

Virgo is a sign you can really rely on. Wherever you have Virgo in your chart (and we all have it somewhere), make like a Virgo and pay proper attention: be fully present to your forgiveness list. Think what life would be like if your heart were free of the upsets you're forgiving this month.

_____

_____

_____

_____

_____

_____

_____

_____

_____

_____

_____

_____

ⵢ Questions to Ask at This Full Moon

Do I understand that gratitude overpowers anxiety? If so, what am I grateful for that I can bring to mind to interrupt anxious feelings?

_____

_____

_____

_____

Have I been worrying myself silly? Where does this worry come from?

_____

_____

_____

_____

Do I need to be more organized? What should my first step be?

_____

_____

_____

_____

FEBRUARY WEEK 9

22 MONDAY   ♊︎♋︎ ◯

23 TUESDAY   ♋︎ ◯

24 WEDNESDAY   ♋︎♌︎ ◯

25 THURSDAY   ♌︎ ◯

○ ♌ ♍   FRIDAY 26

○ ♍   SATURDAY 27

Full Moon
London   08:17
Sydney   19:17
Los Angeles   00:17
New York   03:17

○ ♍ ♎   SUNDAY 28

THIS WEEK

Venus moves into Pisces this month, bringing love and the need for attention. Love affairs that have been perfunctory lately can warm up. See Pisces New Moon, 'What this lunation means for you', section for where Pisces is for you.

March

This month looks like it should unfold fairly smoothly. It kicks off with a lovely connection between loving and abundant Venus and the planet of change, Uranus. So if there's something to do with love or money that you need to turn around, go for it early in the month. There are no guarantees, but at least you know the astrological energies support you.

The quite amazing thing about this March is that if you look at all the astrological alignments for the month ahead (which you can do in an ephemeris), all the major ones are harmonious, with one exception. That's a Mercury/Mars clash we'll start feeling around 24 March. Apart from that, there are lots of intense energies that you can work with. The general message is that the month looks like it's making life a little easier for us all. Go deep without going into fear.

Of special note is the arrival of Mars into Gemini, for the first time in around two years. Wherever Mars goes, increased energy (sometimes frenetic energy, especially in Gemini). follows. We all have Gemini in our chart, so if you want to find out where you're getting this energy boost, see the 'What this lunation means for you' section under New Moon Eclipse in Gemini (*see page 127*). It's the same House.

This month (20 March) also brings what astrologers call 'the Aries Ingress', which is when the Sun moves into the first sign of the zodiac, Aries. This (along with, in my opinion, the Aries New Moon) marks the energetic start of the astrological new year. It's like a free pass to start over.

M	T	W	T	F	S	S
1	2	3	4	5	6	7
8	9	10	11	12	13	14
15	16	17	18	19	20	21
22	23	24	25	26	27	28
29	30	31				

~ Things to do this month ~

1. Forgive the past.
2. Learn to argue nicely and kindly.
3. End a toxic relationship.

MARCH Week 10

1 MONDAY ♎ ○

2 TUESDAY ♎ ♏ ○

3 WEDNESDAY ♏ ○

4 THURSDAY ♏ ♐ ◐

◐ ♐   FRIDAY 5

◑ ♐   SATURDAY 6

What are you grateful for right now?

◑ ♐♑   SUNDAY 7

THIS WEEK

*A few years ago, most people would have written off 'positive
thinking' as hippy era nonsense. But more and more of us have
woken up to the fact that it actually works wonders. This week's
Mercury/Jupiter alignment supports positive thoughts.*

New Moon in Pisces

The key energies of this Moon are:
Dreamy • Romantic • Healing • Mysterious

Place	Date	Time	Degrees
London	13 March	10:21	23:03
Sydney	13 March	21:21	23:03
Los Angeles	13 March	02:21	23:03
New York	13 March	05:21	23:03

This has the potential to be a lovely New Moon. It's in the water sign of Pisces, which is already a good thing in my book. Pisces is the sign of deep dives into life's mysteries and the New Moon here can help us start to access them.

Pisces is the sign that imagines up your life, and it's found in the subconscious part of the astrology chart: the 12th House. That's why it's so important to have a clear subconscious (and why we do Full Moon forgiveness). It's in this part of the chart that many of our deepest dreams are born: from our subconscious. So if we do the Full Moon emotional clear-out every month, via forgiveness, we have a clearer subconscious, rather than one that might be teeming with unresolved anger and resentment.

Moreover, this year's New Moon in Pisces harmonizes with powerful Pluto and is under the influence of a truly dreamy Venus/Neptune alignment. The connection to Pluto gives any wishes you make now extra oomph and power. You can think of Pluto as a powerful blast of volcanic energy that causes seismic change and transformation from the inside out. Any New Moon that connects harmoniously with Pluto is worth tuning in to, so be doubly sure to make your wishes!

Meanwhile, the alignment between Venus and Neptune is potentially delight-*full*. Venus is the planet of love and Neptune the planet of soulmates, so put that together just after the New Moon and you have some wonderful possibilities. That said, if you're involved with someone you don't trust, watch out, and ask yourself *why* you're involved with them.

⚹ What This Lunation Means for You

To discover where the energy of this New Moon is for you, find your Star sign or Rising sign here, see which House is involved, and then read the New Moon through the Houses guide (*see pages 10–14*): Aries – 12th House; Taurus – 11th House; Gemini – 10th House; Cancer – 9th House; Leo – 8th House; Virgo – 7th House; Libra – 6th House; Scorpio – 5th House; Sagittarius – 4th House; Capricorn – 3rd House; Aquarius – 2nd House; Pisces – 1st House.

● Your New Moon Affirmation ●

My life is delightful, and I attract wonderful people into it.

New Moon Wishes and Intentions

Not feeling that you have a good life? There's always *something* to be grateful for. Think of that and hold it in your heart before you make your wishes. And be sure to listen to the New Moon creative visualization meditation at moonmessages.com/diary2021 (In fact, do this every month, even if I don't remind you to.)

_____

_____

_____

_____

_____

_____

_____

_____

_____

_____

_____

Questions to Ask at This New Moon

How am I doing on my spiritual path/development/quest?

_____

_____

_____

_____

Am I meditating as much as I intend to? And if not, why not?
How can I change that?

_____

_____

_____

_____

What's my most romantic dream for my future? Write it down
and feel it as real.

_____

_____

_____

_____

MARCH WEEK 11

8 MONDAY ♑ ◗

9 TUESDAY ♑ ♒ ◗

10 WEDNESDAY ♒ ◖

11 THURSDAY ♒ ♓ ◖

⬤ ♓   FRIDAY 12

⬤ ♓♈   SATURDAY 13

New Moon
London   10:21
Sydney   21:21
Los Angeles 02:21
New York   05:21

⬤ ♈   SUNDAY 14

THIS WEEK

Romance is in the air as we move towards the New Moon in Pisces,
the last New Moon of the current annual lunar cycle (Pisces is the
last sign of the zodiac, and the word of the week is Surrender).

MARCH WEEK 12

....

15 MONDAY   ♈ 🌑

....

16 TUESDAY   ♈♉ 🌑

....

17 WEDNESDAY   ♉ 🌒

....

18 THURSDAY   ♉♊ 🌒

....

 FRIDAY 19

 SATURDAY 20

Spring Equinox/Ostara (northern hemisphere) and
Autumn Equinox/Mabon (southern hemisphere)

 SUNDAY 21

What are you grateful for right now?

THIS WEEK

*Mercury moves into Pisces now, so it's a good time to talk about
whatever Pisces rules in your chart. See 'What this lunation means
for you' for the New Moon in Pisces (see page 71) to find that out.*

Full Moon in Libra

The key energies of this Moon are:
Healing • Commitment • Loving • Poetic

Place	Date	Time	Degrees
London	28 March	19:48	08:18
Sydney	29 March	05:48	08:18
Los Angeles	28 March	01:48	08:18
New York	28 March	14:48	08:18

The Full Moon is taking place in the sign of partnerships and relationships, Libra, and there's also a lot of healing energy in the air. So this week is the time to surrender your relationship issues of any kind to the Divine (*see opposite*).

The great news is that this Full Moon makes a special triangular alignment in the skies called a Grand Trine, which is all about life flowing more easily. Plus, the Sun, loving Venus and healing Chiron are in the same place at the same time.

Because the Full Moon always brings emotions to the surface, there could be some heightened emotions around partnerships and relationships, personal or professional. However, there could also be some deep and loving healing. Remember, life is all about intention, so if you're ready to move on from past upsets with someone (no matter when they took place), now is the time to let them all go.

Mercury, the planet of the mind, and Neptune, the planet of dreams and mysteries, are also together under this Full Moon, making it even more wonderful for surrendering. Surrendering doesn't mean giving up, by the way – it means handing over any issues to the Divine. Trust under the Full Moon.

What This Lunation Means for You

To discover where the energy of this Full Moon is for you, find your Star sign or Rising sign here, see which House is involved, and then read the Full Moon through the Houses guide (*see pages 14–17*): Aries – 7th House; Taurus – 6th House; Gemini – 5th House; Cancer – 4th House; Leo – 3rd House; Virgo – 2nd House; Libra – 1st House; Scorpio – 12th House; Sagittarius – 11th House; Capricorn – 10th House; Aquarius – 9th House; Pisces – 8th House.

Surrender a Relationship to the Divine

Doing this is easier than you might think. On your altar (or a table), put a photo of a person with whom you have a relationship. Raise your vibration with some beautiful music and candles, and drop some essential oil onto your palms (I love Doterra's 'Forgive' as a roll-on). Add a picture of the Libra Goddess Lakshmi or Archangel Jophiel, or an image of anyone you resonate with. Now, with your hands in prayer position, say: 'I surrender my relationship with [name of person] to the Divine. Thank you for guiding me.'

Full Moon Forgiveness List

The Full Moon in Libra is the ideal time to forgive anyone for anything they've ever done. Seriously. It's the Full Moon in the sign of relationships and partnerships, so let it all go. Release resentment. Use the Full Moon Forgiveness and Karma Release Formula (*see page 61*). And then write your forgiveness list and burn it.

_____

_____

_____

_____

_____

_____

_____

_____

_____

_____

Questions to Ask at This Full Moon

Why am I hanging on to anger about what [name of person] did/didn't do to me?

_____

_____

_____

_____

What would love do in this relationship?

_____

_____

_____

_____

Ask yourself these two questions in relation to all your challenged relationships.

_____

_____

_____

_____

MARCH WEEK 13

. . . .

22 MONDAY   ♋ ◗

. . . .

23 TUESDAY   ♋♌ ◗

. . . .

24 WEDNESDAY   ♌ ◗

. . . .

25 THURSDAY   ♌ ◗

. . . .

○♌︎♍︎ FRIDAY 26

○♍︎ SATURDAY 27

○♍︎♎︎ SUNDAY 28

Full Moon
London   19:48
Los Angeles   11:48
New York   14:48

THIS WEEK

*Watch out for saying too much too soon this week, or telling
someone off too harshly, especially around 23 March, when we'll
all be feeling a Mercury (communication)/Mars (anger) clash.*

April

So, here we are at the beginning of the new astrological year. Yes, that's right: this month brings the New Moon in Aries, the first sign of the zodiac, and for me, that marks the start of the new *astrological* year. Other astrologers might argue that the Sun moving into Aries, aka the Aries Ingress, heralds the start of the new year. Whatever you believe, take a moment now to think back over the past 12 months and all that you're grateful for, because a new astrological start is upon us.

The first half of April has the toughest astrology of the month, with a Mars/Neptune clash on the 9th. This can be a time when you're angry and confused. If so, meditate. If you feel you can't sit silently while focusing on your breath (which is essentially what meditation is), listen to some beautiful music on your headphones and just breathe normally.

There's also a Venus/Pluto clash on 12 April, which can see struggles to do with love and money. But more than that, this clash has many implications for us all, and women in particular. It's a time when it can be tough to be female. There's a challenge. Or perhaps a powerful woman is making you squirm? Either way, act consciously.

The other thing about April from an astrological point of view is that it's a second chance new year. So if you've fallen off the wagon with your resolutions for 2021, now's the time to get back on, at the start of the *astrological* new year. Lastly, the Full Moon this month is a Super Full Moon.

M	T	W	T	F	S	S
			1	2	3	4 ◗
5	6	7	8	9	10	11
12 ●	13	14	15	16	17	18
19	20 ◐	21	22	23	24	25
26	27 ○	28	29	30		

~ *Things to do this month* ~

1. Start again.
2. Recommit to your 2021 goals.
3. Make a 12-month plan.

March/April Week 14

---

29 Monday   ♎ ○

Full Moon
Sydney   05:48

---

30 Tuesday   ♎ ♏ ○

---

31 Wednesday   ♏ ○

---

1 Thursday   ♏ ♐ ○

○ ♐   FRIDAY 2

◑ ♐♑   SATURDAY 3

◑ ♑   SUNDAY 4

What are you grateful for right now?

THIS WEEK

A potentially great week, with lots of good energies for
meditating, making solid deals that will last, promises
that you keep, and contracts you come to love.

APRIL WEEK 15

....

5 MONDAY ♑ ♒ ◑

....

6 TUESDAY ♒ ◑

....

7 WEDNESDAY ♒ ♓ ◑

....

8 THURSDAY ♓ ◑

....

Friday 9

◗ ♓

Saturday 10

◗ ♓♈

Sunday 11

● ♈

New Moon
Los Angeles   19:30
New York   22:30

This Week

*There are two lovely Venus links this week – Venus is the
planet of love and abundance, so when she's on good form,
we feel it here on Earth. 'As above, so below'…*

New Moon in Aries

The key energies of this Moon are:
Excitement • Determination • Challenges • Femininity

Place	Date	Time	Degrees
London	12 April	03:30	22:24
Sydney	12 April	12:30	22:24
Los Angeles	11 April	19:30	22:24
New York	11 April	22:30	22:24

As Aries New Moons go, this is an interesting one. On the one hand, it's basically in the same place at the same time as Venus, the planet of love and abundance, and that's a good thing. It suggests some kind of restart connected to love and abundance for us all, but especially for those who choose to tap into the New Moon energy with a simple ritual or ceremony (I'll probably be doing one – check moonmessages.com/fbevents for info).

Venus is also about to clash with Pluto when the New Moon takes place. This could symbolize a year ahead in which women will be fighting for their rights. It could also herald a week in which women are asked to stand up to the patriarchy – to embrace their Goddess consciousness.

The New Moon in Aries is a wonderful time to tune in to Goddess energy. Use your Rising sign to get to know the Goddess who guides you from this list by the amazing Dr Glenys Livingstone, who has a PhD in Goddess studies: Aries – Athena; Taurus – Hathor; Gemini – Saraswati; Cancer (Moonchild) – Selena; Leo – Medusa; Virgo – Ceres; Libra – Lakshmi/Aphrodite; Scorpio – Durga/Kali; Sagittarius – Fortuna; Capricorn – Juno/Hecate; Aquarius – Isis; Pisces – Kuan Yin. Now Google your Goddess, print out her image and commune with her.

Once again, a reminder that Aries is the first sign of the zodiac, so this New Moon marks the start of the new astrological year. If you've bought this diary and are only just tuning in now, don't worry: this is the perfect time to get on board and commit to working with the New and Full Moons of the coming 12 months.

🜨 What This Lunation Means for You

To discover where the energy of this New Moon is for you, find your Star sign or Rising sign here, see which House is involved, and then read the New Moon through the Houses guide (*see pages 10–14*): Aries – 1st House; Taurus – 12th House; Gemini – 11th House; Cancer – 10th House; Leo – 9th House; Virgo – 8th House; Libra – 7th House; Scorpio – 6th House; Sagittarius – 5th House; Capricorn – 4th House; Aquarius – 3rd House; Pisces – 2nd House.

● Your New Moon Affirmation ●

This month I'm renewed. I rise again.

New Moon Wishes and Intentions List

One thing you could wish for this month is a 12-month goal you have in your mind or heart. Aries energy is all about the year ahead, so tap in with at least one long-term wish. Stuck for what to wish for? Wish to make New Moon wishes every month. Wish for world peace! Intention is everything.

Questions to Ask at This New Moon

What do I want for the coming 12 months?

_____

_____

_____

_____

Am I willing to commit to 12 months of New Moon wishes and intentions?

_____

_____

_____

_____

What does it mean to be female in 2021? (Ask this regardless of your gender).

_____

_____

_____

_____

APRIL WEEK 16

....

12 MONDAY

New Moon
London   03:30
Sydney   12:30

....

13 TUESDAY

....

14 WEDNESDAY

....

15 THURSDAY

....

FRIDAY 16

SATURDAY 17

SUNDAY 18

THIS WEEK

This week looks like it's going to get better as each day unfurls. The New Moon phase lasts around three days, so feel free to delay your wishes until a few hours (at least two) after the New Moon.

APRIL WEEK 17

....

19 MONDAY   ♋ ☽

....

20 TUESDAY   ♋♌ ☽

What are you grateful for right now?
....

21 WEDNESDAY   ♌ ☽

....

22 THURSDAY   ♌♍ ☽

....

◯ ♍   FRIDAY 23

....

◯ ♍ ♎   SATURDAY 24

....

◯ ♎   SUNDAY 25

....

THIS WEEK

*This week brings the possible changes and turnarounds to
do with love and abundance I mentioned a while ago. Not
happy about something to do with either of these topics?
Tell the Universe that you want positive change!*

Super Full Moon in Scorpio

The key energies of this Moon are:
Volatile • Passionate • Deep • Communicative

Place	Date	Time	Degrees
London	27 April	04:31	07:06
Sydney	27 April	13:31	07:06
Los Angeles	26 April	20:31	07:06
New York	26 April	23:31	07:06

We can expect pretty high energies this lunation as it's a Super Full Moon. Supermoons occur when the Moon is at Her closest point to Earth in Her monthly orbit. A Super Full Moon will look up to 14 per cent larger and 30 per cent brighter than a Full Moon. In her book *The Bond*, Lynne McTaggart notes that some scientists have suggested that the placement of the Moon 'amplifies or muffles the geomagnetic pull of the Sun and the Earth's geomagnetic field'.

In astrology, the Moon symbolizes emotions, so they swell with the Moon at Full Moon time. Add to this the fact that Scorpio is a super-intense sign; and to top it off, the Full Moon clashes with Saturn and hits mayhem planet Uranus.

This is a Full Moon to go into consciously. We're all full of the hopes and dreams we unleashed into the Universe at the time of the most recent New Moon. So how are your dreams looking? Have you acted on them? Complete the Dreams Check up exercise below.

Additionally, Scorpio is a dark sign (we all have it in our chart somewhere), so use the energies to release darkness and grudges. Can you forgive someone you've been angry with for too long? If so, it'll change your life.

What This Lunation Means for You

To discover where the energy of this Full Moon is for you, find your Star sign or Rising sign here, see which House is involved, and then read the Full Moon through the Houses guide (*see pages 14–17*): Aries – 8th House; Taurus – 7th House; Gemini – 6th House; Cancer – 5th House; Leo – 4th House; Virgo – 3rd House; Libra – 2nd House; Scorpio – 1st House; Sagittarius – 12th House; Capricorn – 11th House; Aquarius – 10th House; Pisces – 9th House.

Dreams Checkup

Take a look at the wishes and intentions list you made at the New Moon in Aries (*see page 92*). That's the beauty of a diary like this: you can see the intentions you've set – which is why it's 100 per cent worth doing them every month. Now check whether you've done what you said you'd do. If not, are you willing to release resistance to it under this Full Moon? Say it out loud on Full Moon night: 'I release resistance to making my dreams come true.'

Full Moon Forgiveness List

Forgiveness really can change your life. This is a super-good Full Moon to work with forgiveness, because it's in the grudge-holding sign of Scorpio (which we all have in our chart somewhere). So, work extra hard at forgiving someone you've never forgiven before. Maybe someone you've been mad with for ages... decades, even. Go on, you can do it.

_____

_____

_____

_____

_____

_____

_____

_____

_____

_____

⚳ Questions to Ask at This Full Moon

Which grudges do I need to release?

_____

_____

_____

_____

Can I find it in my heart to forgive [name of person]? What soul lessons did they teach me when they hurt me? Were they worthwhile lessons?

_____

_____

_____

_____

Do I understand that forgiveness is as much for my own good as anything else? How does this idea make me feel?

_____

_____

_____

_____

APRIL WEEK 18

26 MONDAY ♎ ♏ ○

Super Full Moon
Los Angeles   20:31
New York   23:31

27 TUESDAY ♏ ○

Super Full Moon
London   04:31
Sydney   13:31

28 WEDNESDAY ♏ ♐ ○

29 THURSDAY ♐ ○

◯ ♐♑   FRIDAY 30

◯ ♑   SATURDAY 1

Festivals of Beltane (northern hemisphere) and
Samhain (southern hemisphere)

◯ ♑ ♒   SUNDAY 2

THIS WEEK

*Confusion and weirdness around love and money
early on in the week can be resolved nicely by the end
of it. The trick is to be honest and optimistic.*

May

The big news is that May is an eclipse month. More details about this coming up, but on 26 May, it's a Full Moon eclipse in the sign of Sagittarius all over the world. In other words, we're now moving into a new eclipse season. Are you ready?

The way to prepare for the eclipse season is simply to get clear about what you do and don't want. Once you've isolated what you want to release – which is the best thing to do at Full Moon – doing so will actually start, and the work you do at the Full Moon (for which I'll give you ideas) will just make the process faster and hopefully easier.

The other equally important news is that this month, Jupiter – which has been in the sign of Aquarius for all of 2021 so far – moves into Pisces. Jupiter is the planet of plenty so his move into Pisces means you're about to get lucky in a whole new part of your chart.

To find out where Pisces is in your chart, go to the New or Full Moon in Pisces section and read 'What this lunation means for you'. Whichever House is given, it's the same House, so look up the meaning in the New Moon and Full Moon through the Houses guides (*see pages 10–17*). That's where you have extra good luck now, thanks to fortuitous

Jupiter in this part of your chart for the next few months. Also note that Mercury goes retrograde on 29/30 May (depending on where you are in the world). This time around, Mercury is doing so in the sign of Gemini.

M	T	W	T	F	S	S
					1	2
3 ◐	4	5	6	7	8	9
10	11 ●	12	13	14	15	16
17	18	19 ◑	20	21	22	23
24	25	26 ○	27	28	29	30
31						

～ Things to do this month ～

1. Change your luck.
2. Let go of the past.
3. Reconstruct your life.

MAY WEEK 19

. . . .

3 MONDAY ♒ ◗

What are you grateful for right now?
. . . .

4 TUESDAY ♒ ◗

. . . .

5 WEDNESDAY ♒♓ ◗

. . . .

6 THURSDAY ♓ ◗

. . . .

●)⚹♈   FRIDAY 7

●)♈   SATURDAY 8

●)♈♉   SUNDAY 9

THIS WEEK

*There's a tough link between the Sun and Saturn now,
so if you find yourself lecturing someone, draw a breath
and consider backing off. Someone lecturing you? Breathe
deep! There may be a good lesson in it for you.*

New Moon in Taurus

The key energies of this Moon are:
Excitement • Motivation • Abundance • Inspiration

Place	Date	Time	Degrees
London	11 May	19:59	21:17
Sydney	12 May	04.59	21:17
Los Angeles	11 May	11:59	21:17
New York	11 May	14:59	21:17

This looks like a very positive New Moon, you'll be glad to hear. It's in the sign of Taurus, which is all about abundance, among other things. If you're making your New Moon wishes every month then well done, you. This New Moon is a great one for intentions. It opens up an abundance portal, so to speak, so there's a chance to create a new level of prosperity. This particular New Moon in Taurus has extra 'astrological medicine' to offer as it's connected to the planet of the Divine, Neptune. Already that's a good thing. It elevates the energies. The. Planet. Of. The. Divine.

So, meditate your way through this if you want to create more cash. We're all able to tap into prosperity – we just need to know that we're worth it.

Taurus rules the 2nd House on the 'natural' astrology chart, and as such it's a great time to check in on your self-worth. No one is going to advise you to overrate yourself, but do rate yourself highly – then others will do the same. As you make your wishes, tap into your self-worth and see if you need to value yourself (or someone else) a little more from here on in.

⚛ What This Lunation Means for You

To discover where the energy of this New Moon is for you, find your Star sign or Rising sign here, see which House is involved, and then read the New Moon through the Houses guide (*see pages 10–14*): Aries – 2nd House; Taurus – 1st House; Gemini – 12th House; Cancer – 11th House; Leo – 10th House; Virgo – 9th House; Libra – 8th House; Scorpio – 7th House; Sagittarius – 6th House; Capricorn – 5th House; Aquarius – 4th House; Pisces – 3rd House.

⚛ Connect with the Goddess of Abundance

Taurus is ruled by Venus, and my favourite Goddess associated with Venus is the Hindu Lakshmi. She's part of a triple Goddess known as Narayani and represents, among other things, abundance, love and motherhood. Google her, print out her picture and listen to the chant for this New Moon at my site (moonmessages.com/diary2021).

● Your New Moon Affirmation ●

*An abundance portal is opening up to
me and I'm walking through it.*

New Moon Wishes and Intentions List

This is the month to make some proper wishes about money, abundance, prosperity... or whatever you want to call it. If you feel blessed financially already, then wish to be generous; if you're already generous, wish to be more generous. We're here to create comfortable lives for ourselves and others – it's part of the human experience in 3D. It's okay.

_____

_____

_____

_____

_____

_____

_____

_____

_____

_____

_____

_____

_____

Questions to Ask at This New Moon

What represents abundance to me? What would it look like for me?

_____

_____

_____

_____

Am I generous, with myself and others? Who do I love who is generous? How does their generosity make me feel?

_____

_____

_____

_____

What do I really value and am I living my life in accordance with that?

_____

_____

_____

_____

MAY WEEK 20

10 MONDAY

11 TUESDAY

New Moon
London   19:59
Los Angeles   11:59
New York   14:59

12 WEDNESDAY

New Moon
Sydney   04:59

13 THURSDAY

◐ ♊   FRIDAY 14

◐ ♊♋   SATURDAY 15

◐ ♋   SUNDAY 16

THIS WEEK

*This is a big week because the planet Jupiter
is making a move from Aquarius (where it's
been for the past year or so) into Pisces.*

MAY WEEK 21

17 MONDAY ♋ ♌ ☽

18 TUESDAY ♌ ☽

19 WEDNESDAY ♌ ♍ ☽

What are you grateful for right now?

20 THURSDAY ♍ ☽

☽ ♍ FRIDAY 21

☽ ♍ ♎ SATURDAY 22

☽ ♎ SUNDAY 23

THIS WEEK

There is some super-positive Venus action this week (Venus harmonizes with healing Chiron and committed Saturn) so expect good things regarding love and abundance..

Super Full Moon Eclipse in Sagittarius

The key energies of this Moon are:
Turnarounds • Liberation • Releasing • Crumbling

Place	Date	Time	Degrees
London	26 May	12:13	05:25
Sydney	26 May	21:13	05:25
Los Angeles	26 May	04:13	05:25
New York	26 May	07:13	05:25

Expect a pretty big week with lots of room for confusion. And, it has to be said, possibly some deception. There are times in life when events conspire to show us that someone isn't on the level. When that happens, we have a few choices: pretend it's not real, or tackle the issue.

This week's eclipse in Sagittarius could be a little bit confused or deceptive because there's a challenging Mercury/Venus clash with confusing Neptune around at the same time. The good news is that a few days after this Mercury/Venus/Neptune clash, Mercury goes on to harmonize with Venus.

The message here is that even if life feels a bit rough, especially where a matter related to love or money is concerned, don't give up. In the fullness of time, you'll start to see why what happened *had* to happen. An example would be breaking up with someone who broke your heart, which makes space for the right person to come into your life.

Also note that Mercury goes retrograde this week, so whatever happens now could have a second chance later.

⚹ What This Lunation Means for You

To discover where the energy of this Full Moon is for you, find your Star sign or Rising sign here, see which House is involved, and then read the Full Moon through the Houses guide (*see pages 14–17*): Aries – 9th House; Taurus – 8th House; Gemini – 7th House; Cancer – 6th House; Leo – 5th House; Virgo – 4th House; Libra – 3rd House; Scorpio – 2nd House; Sagittarius – 1st House; Capricorn – 12th House; Aquarius – 11th House; Pisces – 10th House.

⚹ A 'Letting Go' Ceremony for the Eclipse

Every Full Moon brings the chance to release, but a Full Moon eclipse brings that *plus plus*. Try this technique:

1. On a piece of paper, write about something difficult in your life that you want to release. Allow yourself a good 30 minutes and write until you feel that you've really unpacked every detail. Depending on the seriousness of the issue, you might even start to see it in a new light.

2. Now burn what you've written to release the difficulty and you'll start to see it in a new light.

Full Moon Forgiveness List

Just as this eclipse is extra useful for letting go of the 'stuff' that bungs you up and stops you from feeling good and manifesting easily, it's also excellent for supercharged forgiveness. So, along with writing your forgiveness list, recite the Formula for Forgiveness and Karma Release (*see page 61*) on the night of the Full Moon. Don't miss this opportunity.

_____

_____

_____

_____

_____

_____

_____

_____

_____

_____

_____

⚹ Questions to Ask at This Full Moon

What do I need to release?

_____

_____

_____

_____

What is the pay-off or benefit for _not_ releasing it?

_____

_____

_____

_____

Am I willing to let it go and move on?

_____

_____

_____

_____

_____

MAY WEEK 22

24 MONDAY

♎ ♏ ○

25 TUESDAY

♏ ○

26 WEDNESDAY

♏ ♐ ○

Super Full Moon Eclipse
London   12:13
Sydney   21:13
Los Angeles   04:13
New York   07:13

27 THURSDAY

♐ ○

....

○ ♐♑   FRIDAY **28**

....

○ ♑   SATURDAY **29**

Mercury goes retrograde (until 22 June).
....

○ ♑♒   SUNDAY **30**

....

THIS WEEK

Communication planet Mercury goes retrograde in the sign
of Gemini this week, which could cause a lot of confusion,
since Gemini is the communication sign. Humour is the
key to surviving this. The cycle lasts until 22 June.

June

Wow, so here we are – midyear, already. In the northern hemisphere, people are getting ready to enjoy summer, and Down Under they're hunkering down for the winter.

Did you know that the seasons are based on astrology, more or less? In the northern hemisphere, spring traditionally sprang on or around March 21 or 22, aka the day of the 'Aries Ingress', or the day when the Sun moved into the astrological sign of Aries, the first sign of the zodiac. Down Under, because the seasons are reversed, it marks the start of autumn. It's the same for summer starting in the northern hemisphere this month, and winter starting in the southern hemisphere. Amazing, right?

Of course, these days, in some parts of the world, 'they' say that summer starts on 1 June (northern hemisphere) or 1 December (southern hemisphere) – all very perfunctory. This makes me sigh. For me, it's really not too far out to say that the mindset that succeeded to a large degree in separating women from their power during The Burning Years is the same one that ignores the planet's rhythms and seasons and declares: 'Henceforth, summer starts now, because we say so!'

Even if you're told it's summer or winter where you live at the start of this month, make a mental note that this time around, summer/winter/the Cancer Ingress is *actually* on 21 June, no matter where you are in the world. Oh, and there's an eclipse this month.

M	T	W	T	F	S	S
	1	2 ◑	3	4	5	6
7	8	9	10 ●	11	12	13
14	15	16	17	18 ◐	19	20
21	22	23	24 ○	25	26	27
28	29	30				

~ Things to do this month ~

1. Celebrate the changing of the season.
2. Change your life.
3. Make sense of life again.

MAY/JUNE WEEK 23

31 MONDAY ♒ ◑

1 TUESDAY ♒♓ ◑

2 WEDNESDAY ♓ ◑

What are you grateful for right now?

3 THURSDAY ♓♈ ◑

Friday 4

Saturday 5

Sunday 6

This Week

This is the week before the New Moon eclipse, so take some time to let go of what no longer feels right; also, feel grateful for all that's good, and think about what you want to bring into your life.

New Moon Eclipse in Gemini

The key energies of this Moon are:
Restarts • Quests • Limitations • Breakthroughs

Place	Date	Time	Degrees
London	10 June	11:52	19:47
Sydney	10 June	20:52	19:47
Los Angeles	10 June	03:52	19:47
New York	10 June	06:52	19:47

This is a very interesting and slightly weird eclipse. It's in the fluid sign of Gemini, just as the latest of the round of Saturn/Uranus clashes takes place. Does this mean it's all bad? No way. However, it's definitely a time to live consciously and intentionally. Neptune, the numinous planet, gives us access to the Divine – but under this lunation it's clashing confusingly with the Moon, Sun and Mercury.

Move through any confusion this week with a daily practice that'll connect you with your Higher Self and basically transform your life. In fact, one of the best ways to work through this eclipse clash with Neptune is to think about your spirituality and where you are with it. How? Just meditate daily, or chant.

The Saturn/Uranus clash is a follow-up, or a kind of cosmic echo, of the Uranus/Pluto clashes from 2011 to 2015. There's a good chance that we're all being asked whether we made the life changes we already knew we needed during this period. Enjoy the ride!

I'd highly recommend a spot of journalling under this eclipse. Gemini is associated with writing, and journalling really helps us to express our stuff. Just remember to make your New Moon eclipse wishes, too.

✳ Just say Ommm

The planet Neptune being triggered by the eclipse this week is strongly associated with music. And chanting is music. Silent chanting is even more powerful than chanting out loud. Holding crystals at the same time could elevate your experience. Start by chanting 'Ommm' or 'Peace'.

✳ What This Lunation Means for You

To discover where the energy of this New Moon is for you, find your Star sign or Rising sign here, see which House is involved, and then read the New Moon through the Houses guide (*see pages 10–14*): Aries – 3rd House; Taurus – 2nd House; Gemini – 1st House; Cancer – 12th House; Leo – 11th House; Virgo – 10th House; Libra – 9th House; Scorpio – 8th House; Sagittarius – 7th House; Capricorn – 6th House; Aquarius – 5th House; Pisces – 4th House.

● Your New Moon Affirmation ●

I'm living consciously and intentionally.

New Moon Wishes and Intentions List

Of course, there's no better time to write down wishes and intentions than at a New Moon, let alone at a New Moon eclipse, let alone at a New Moon eclipse in the writing sign of Gemini. It's a confusing and intense time. Maybe this will help. Be honest: how confident do you feel about what you're writing down?

_____

_____

_____

_____

_____

_____

_____

_____

_____

_____

_____

_____

⚹ Questions to Ask at This New Moon

Am I willing to do whatever it takes to get clear about my life? What is my first best step (you intuitively know this)?

_____

_____

_____

_____

Have I been thinking straight, and if not, why not?

_____

_____

_____

_____

Who do I need to talk to?

_____

_____

_____

_____

JUNE WEEK 24

....

7 MONDAY   ♉ ◐

....

8 TUESDAY   ♉♊ ◑

....

9 WEDNESDAY   ♊ ◑

....

10 THURSDAY   ♊ ●

New Moon Eclipse
London   11:52
Sydney   20:52
Los Angeles   03:52
New York   06:52

....

● ♊♋   FRIDAY 11

● ♋   SATURDAY 12

● ♋♌   SUNDAY 13

THIS WEEK

If you feel confused about your New Moon wishes now, or about life in general, thank the stars. Go easy on yourself! Join me for a free online ceremony at moonmessages.com/fbevents, if you wish.

JUNE WEEK 25

....

14 MONDAY ♌ 🌔

....

15 TUESDAY ♌ 🌔

....

16 WEDNESDAY ♌♍ 🌔

....

17 THURSDAY ♍ 🌓

....

☽ ♍︎ ♎︎   FRIDAY 18

What are you grateful for right now?

☽ ♎︎   SATURDAY 19

☽ ♎︎ ♏︎   SUNDAY 20

THIS WEEK

This is the actual week of the Saturn/Uranus clash; before
was the lead-up and now the alignment perfects on 14 June.
Aim for lasting, extensive transformation in your life.
What would that look like for you? It's never too late.

Full Moon in Capricorn

The key energies of this Moon are:
Effort • Healing • Seeking • Completion

Place	Date	Time	Degrees
London	24 June	19:39	03:27
Sydney	25 June	04:39	03:27
Los Angeles	24 June	11:39	03:27
New York	24 June	14:39	03:27

The good news is that by the time we get this Full Moon, we're (a) out of eclipse season and (b) through the latest Saturn/Uranus clash. This means we can all draw breath. However, make no mistake, we're dealing with the aftermath of all that now too. It can be a tense time, especially if you don't look after yourself. So treat yourself this month – a candlelit bath laced with oils and/or salts, music, meditation, and so on. You deserve it.

Also, this Full Moon is in the sign of Capricorn, straddling the opposite sign of Cancer. This axis is about work versus family, so use this Full Moon to think about how you're dealing with that in your life. Working mothers will always have some guilt about not giving their kids (and partner) the time they deserve, *or* being decisive about getting home on time and missing out on opportunities at work because they're seen as too invested in their private life. This applies to working fathers too, of course.

So this month, try to strike a better balance. The Full Moon brings up the tug-of-war – all the better to force us working parents to deal with it! It's also a good week for hard work, and if you're signing off on a big work project, you're doing it at the right time.

What This Lunation Means for You

To discover where the energy of this Full Moon is for you, find your Star sign or Rising sign here, see which House is involved, and then read the Full Moon through the Houses guide (*see pages 14–17*): Aries – 10th House; Taurus – 9th House; Gemini – 8th House; Cancer – 7th House; Leo – 6th House; Virgo – 5th House; Libra – 4th House; Scorpio – 3rd House; Sagittarius – 2nd House; Capricorn – 1st House; Aquarius – 12th House; Pisces – 11th House.

What Turnarounds Do You Want?

The first alignment the Moon makes after the Full Moon is a harmonious one to the planet of change and excitement, Uranus. Use this to shake off any strangeness you've been feeling: change your vibe; go for a walk outside; cleanse your home with smoke. Decide on the change that you want and go for it. We're now out of the eclipse season, so life should settle down. B-r-e-a-t-h-e. If it helps, share your goals with a friend.

Full Moon Forgiveness List

The past few weeks have been pretty intense, so if you've felt stressed and lost your cool, with yourself or someone else, that's okay! That's what the Full Moon is for – maybe that's why the Universe invented it: so we can feel all our feelings as they come up, and process them and then... forgive them.

Questions to Ask at This Full Moon

Am I working too hard (or not enough)? Am I working hard enough to achieve my goals?

_____

_____

_____

_____

Am I living in integrity with my beliefs? If so, how? And if not, why not?

_____

_____

_____

_____

Do I need to give myself or someone else a break? Who?

_____

_____

_____

_____

JUNE WEEK 26

....

21 MONDAY   ♏⚲ ☽

Summer Solstice/Litha (northern hemisphere);
Winter Solstice/Yule (southern hemisphere)
....

22 TUESDAY   ♏⚲ ♐ ☽

Mercury retrograde ends.
....

23 WEDNESDAY   ♐ ☽

....

24 THURSDAY   ♐ ♑ ○

Full Moon
London   19:39
Los Angeles   11:39
New York   14:39

....

○ ♑

FRIDAY 25

Full Moon
Sydney   04:39

○ ♑ ♒

SATURDAY 26

○ ♒

SUNDAY 27

THIS WEEK

*Mercury goes 'direct' this week. This means that Mercury
retrograde is finally ending, although the shadow lasts until
7 July. All those confused and/or second thoughts you've had
could (maybe should) start to inform your next move... or not.*

July

Probably the biggest news this month is that the planet of plenty, Jupiter, which is currently retrograde, moves back into Aquarius until December. This is especially good for anyone born late in the Leo or Aquarius period. It's also good news for all the Fire and Air signs, so Aries and Sagittarius, Gemini and Libra as well.

All this said, it's not actually bad news for anyone: Jupiter is known as the Great Benefic and it basically brings good luck to everyone as it goes around the skies. Think of Jupiter as Father Christmas, or that wonderful uncle with a red nose from lots of good cheer. Jupiter reversing basically gives you second chances to get lucky, to see the bigger picture and/ or to travel, study, teach or expand your life philosophies.

To work out where Jupiter is now bringing you luck (which House on your chart), check the New Moon in Aquarius 'What this lunation means for you' section (*see page 53*). The House given there is the House that Aquarius rules in your chart. This is one of those times when you'd do really well to read your Rising sign, since you have the chance to find out where you're getting lucky for the next six months. If you don't know your Rising sign, find it for free at my site (moonmessages.com/freechart).

If you'd like to improve your luck, have a chat with the goddess of good fortune, prosperity and luck, Fortuna. Simply print out a picture of Fortuna from the Internet and put it on your altar, mantelpiece or dressing table, and then... chat.

M	T	W	T	F	S	S
			1 ◗	2	3	4
5	6	7	8	9	10 ●	11
12	13	14	15	16	17 ◗	18
19	20	21	22	23	24 ○	25
26	27	28	29	30	31 ◗	

~ Things to do this month ~

1. Get lucky (again).
2. Go digital.
3. B-r-e-a-t-h-e!

JUNE/JULY WEEK 27

....

28 MONDAY   ♒︎ ♓︎ ☽

....

29 TUESDAY   ♓︎ ☽

....

30 WEDNESDAY   ♓︎ ☽

....

1 THURSDAY   ♓︎ ♈︎ ☽

What are you grateful for right now?
....

◐ ♈   FRIDAY 2

◐ ♈♉   SATURDAY 3

◐ ♉   SUNDAY 4

THIS WEEK

There's a lot of Mars action this week and not all of it is
harmonious. It's a time to chase your dreams, but be sure
you don't ride roughshod over someone while doing it.

New Moon in Cancer

The key energies of this Moon are:
Shedding • Sexiness • Homeliness • Dynamism

Place	Date	Time	Degrees
London	10 July	02:16	18:01
Sydney	10 July	11:16	18:01
Los Angeles	9 July	18:16	18:01
New York	9 July	21:16	18:01

After last month's slightly weird New Moon eclipse in Gemini, you'll be pleased to hear that this New Moon in Cancer is a bit more rational and orderly. For one thing, this time around, the New Moon is making a harmonious link to the planet of dreams and soulmates, Neptune. This is a gift from the heavens, for sure. If you want to really tap into this lunation, meditate your way through it.

Cancer may have a rep for being crabby and moody, *but* it's also the sign of the home and family (where let's be honest, people can sometimes be a little crabby and moody). So if you have intentions you want to send out to the Universe about your home and/or family life, this is the New Moon to make your wishes and commitments.

Also know that the first alignment after the New Moon is a rather lovely one between Venus and Mars. If there are strained relations between you and a member of the opposite sex, now is the time to put 'a smoother relationship with x' on your wishes list.

Remember, at least half the reason why New Moon wishes work is because they're about intention setting. As I said earlier, try to avoid the habit of simply jotting down your wishes and thinking that's enough to make them come true. Instead, take your #1 New Moon wish for the month and turn it into an affirmation – in other words, write it down as if it's *already real*, then *feel* it as real as you say it out loud with gusto and passion. *That's* how you make your wishes come true.

Listen to the creative visualization meditation at moonmessages.com/diary2021 to help you with this.

⚹ What this Lunation Means for You

To discover where the energy of this New Moon is for you, find your Star sign or Rising sign here, see which House is involved, and then read the New Moon through the Houses guide (*see pages 10–14*): Aries – 4th House; Taurus – 3rd House; Gemini – 2nd House; Cancer – 1st House; Leo – 12th House; Virgo – 11th House; Libra – 10th House; Scorpio – 9th House; Sagittarius – 8th House; Capricorn – 7th House; Aquarius – 6th House; Pisces – 5th House.

● Your New Moon Affirmation ●

My loved ones and I are safe, and for that I'm grateful.

New Moon Wishes and Intentions List

If you want to make some wishes in line with this New Moon, think about your family and home life. What improvement would you like to see in these parts of your life in the coming 12 months? This is also a good New Moon to make wishes about love and money, and to recommit to a powerful spiritual practice.

_____

_____

_____

_____

_____

_____

_____

_____

_____

_____

_____

Questions to Ask at This New Moon

What can I do to improve my home life?

_____

_____

_____

_____

What would a more robust spiritual practice do for me?

_____

_____

_____

_____

Can I spend more time visualizing my goals and feeling them as real? How many minutes a day am I willing to commit to it?

_____

_____

_____

_____

JULY WEEK 28

....

5 MONDAY ♉︎ 🌓

....

6 TUESDAY ♉︎♊︎ 🌓

....

7 WEDNESDAY ♊︎ 🌓

....

8 THURSDAY ♊︎♋︎ 🌔

....

New Moon

FRIDAY 9

New Moon
Los Angeles   18:16
New York   21:16

New Moon

SATURDAY 10

New Moon
London   02:16
Sydney   11:16

SUNDAY 11

THIS WEEK

*There's a weird Mercury/Neptune clash that could be a
bit confusing this week, but apart from that, it looks quite
promising as we move towards the New Moon.*

JULY WEEK 29

....

12 MONDAY   ♌ ◗

....

13 TUESDAY   ♌♍ ◗

....

14 WEDNESDAY   ♍ ◗

....

15 THURSDAY   ♍♎ ◗

....

◐♎   FRIDAY 16

. . . .

◐♎♏   SATURDAY 17

What are you grateful for right now?
. . . .

◐♏   SUNDAY 18

. . . .

THIS WEEK

*This really could be a rather wonderful week, thanks to some lovely
planetary alignments, including mind planet Mercury harmonizing
with confident Jupiter. Make the most of it. Expect good things!*

Full Moon in Aquarius

The key energies of this Moon are:
Karma • Maturing • Lessons • Commitment

Place	Date	Time	Degrees
London	24 July	03:36	01:26
Sydney	24 July	12:36	01:26
Los Angeles	23 July	19:36	01:26
New York:	23 July	22:36	01:26

This is a bit of a mixed bag of a Full Moon, stuck between eruptive Pluto and hard-bitten Saturn. In ancient astrology this wouldn't have been regarded as a good thing; however, in modern astrology, it's seen as a chance to have a life clear-out and then put some new structures in place.

Very nicely, the nearest alignment after the Full Moon is between mind planet Mercury and numinous Neptune. In other words, if you're on a spiritual path, you have a lovely chance to really go higher with your spiritual practice at the Full Moon time and in the coming month. Meditation, chanting, yoga and journalling will work a treat. Remember to check moonmessages.com/fbevents to join me for my Full Moon ceremony.

This Full Moon is also good for the traditional letting go and forgiving. It's in Aquarius, so at some level you can detach yourself from the past and move on. Very often, as with most things, it's all about intention. So when you do your Full Moon work, try to feel as detached as you can from whomever you're forgiving. It'll make things easier.

There's also a lovely Mercury/Pluto alignment building that'll help make space for powerful conversations, if that's something you need to make happen. Note this is the first of two Aquarius Full Moons in a row.

⚹ What This Lunation Means for You

To discover where the energy of this Full Moon is for you, find your Star sign or Rising sign here, see which House is involved, and then read the Full Moon through the Houses guide (*see pages 14–17*): Aries – 11th House; Taurus – 10th House; Gemini – 9th House; Cancer – 8th House; Leo – 7th House; Virgo – 6th House; Libra – 5th House; Scorpio – 4th House; Sagittarius – 3rd House; Capricorn – 2nd House; Aquarius – 1st House; Pisces – 12th House.

⚹ Tap into Mercury

Mercury is the most active planet this week, so it's a great time to get in touch with the Mercury energies. The message from Mercury is to improve our communication within our limited abilities of speech, writing and sign language. We need to express ourselves. If you want to connect with Mercury's energy, listen to the Saraswati chant at moonmessages.com/diary2021. Saraswati is the Goddess of language and is therefore associated with Mercury.

Full Moon Forgiveness List

The intensity of this Full Moon is likely to bring quite a few feelings to the surface – all the better for you to process them. Resistance is the force that stops us from manifesting our dreams, so look at where you've been resisting and forgive yourself and others. Note below what resistance you're releasing and where you're forgiving.

_____

_____

_____

_____

_____

_____

_____

_____

_____

_____

_____

_____

_____

⚴ Questions to Ask at This Full Moon

Where do I feel boxed in? Am I imagining it?

_____

_____

_____

_____

Am I communicating as well as I should? With whom could I communicate better, and what effect would that have?

_____

_____

_____

_____

Where is my energy best spent?

_____

_____

_____

_____

JULY WEEK 30

....

19 MONDAY   ♏ ♐ ☽

....

20 TUESDAY   ♐ ☽

....

21 WEDNESDAY   ♐ ♑ ○

....

22 THURSDAY   ♑ ○

....

○ ♑

FRIDAY 23

Full Moon
Los Angeles   19:36
New York   22:36

○ ♑ ♒

SATURDAY 24

Full Moon
London   03:36
Sydney   12:36

○ ♒

SUNDAY 25

THIS WEEK

*It's all about communication this week, and also about love. If you keep
the lines of communication open, then your love life and other important
love relationships (such as family and friends) should go pretty well.*

JULY WEEK 31

....

26 MONDAY   ♒ ♓ ◑

....

27 TUESDAY   ♓ ◑

....

28 WEDNESDAY   ♓ ♈ ◐

....

29 THURSDAY   ♈ ◑

....

◐ ♈ ♉   Friday 30

◐ ♉   Saturday 31

What are you grateful for right now?

◐ ♉   Sunday 1

Festivals of Lammas (northern hemisphere)
and Imbolc (southern hemisphere)

This Week

*This is the week that lucky planet Jupiter slips back into
the sign of Aquarius for one last hurrah. Expect second
chances and lucky breaks the second time around.*

August

It's a fairly quiet month astrologically, with few major alignments to speak of. Does that mean nothing special is going to happen? Not at all. But it does suggest that life should be slightly less up and down. One of the major themes at the moment is reconstructing and rebuilding life. So, rather than trying to forge ahead with everything, use August to see where you are, and check if you're happy with where you're going.

The planet Saturn is currently retrograde; in fact, Saturn is retrograde nearly five months every year. Think of Saturn as the 'building blocks' planet, so when it's moving forwards, the pressure is on to build something new and solid in your life. And when Saturn is retrograde (going 'backwards'), as it is now, it can be a time to pull down structures that aren't sturdy and need rebuilding. The energies for Saturn include constructing, so the retrograde is often about reconstructing.

Saturn is currently retrograde in the sign of Aquarius. To find out what that means for you – in other words, which part of your life Aquarius rules – see 'What this lunation means for you' for Full Moon in Aquarius (*see page 153*). Whichever House the Full Moon is affecting, that's the House ruled by Aquarius in your chart. Since Saturn is in

Aquarius now, it's affecting the same part of your chart, so you're getting some intense action there.

Also, this month's Full Moon is known as a Blue Moon as it's the third Full Moon in a season with four Full Moons.

M	T	W	T	F	S	S
						1
2	3	4	5	6	7	8 ●
9	10	11	12	13	14	15 ◑
16	17	18	19	20	21	22 ○
23	24	25	26	27	28	29
30 ◑	31					

~ Things to do this month ~

1. Believe in the impossible!
2. Let go of the past more easily.
3. Transform your finances.

New Moon in Leo

The key energies of this Moon are:
Communication • Excess • Romance • Prosperity

Place	Date	Time	Degrees
London	8 August	14:50	16:14
Sydney	8 August	23:50	16:14
Los Angeles	8 August	06:50	16:14
New York	8 August	09:50	16:14

The New Moon in Leo is as bright and confident as the sign itself. As you probably know, the sign of Leo is represented by the Sun, around which all the planets rotate. The Sun is, of course, the Giver of Life. Some mystics I've spoken to, or whose work I've read, even say that the Sun *is* God! This makes a strange kind of sense when you think of (a) the majesty of the Sun, (b) the fact the Sun sustains us, and (c) the idea of Sun worship, which we humans innately do. Since Leo is ruled by the Sun, all these ideas (and more). should be taken into account when thinking about the sign itself, and the New Moon in this sign.

This year, the New Moon in Leo is taking place right near Mercury, the communication planet, which happens to be aligned with Jupiter, the over-the-top planet. This adds up to a good New Moon if you want to better express yourself, you need the confidence to tell someone how you feel, or need to be reminded of your own magnificence.

 ## Re-storying Medusa

Did you know that the Goddess Medusa – the Scary One – is often associated with the Sun? Her magical snake hair (representing feminine wisdom) makes her look like a Sun Goddess, and indeed, many Goddess scholars refer to her as one. Medusa is one of the most powerful and misunderstood Goddesses. Her decapitation represents the decapitation of the matriarchy by the patriarchy. See if you dare connect to her this month. Print out her picture from moonmessages. com/medusa. Meditate with her and see what she reveals to you. Write it down.

 ## What This Lunation Means for You

To discover where the energy of this New Moon is for you, find your Star sign or Rising sign here, see which House is involved, and then read the New Moon through the Houses guide (*see pages 10–14*): Aries – 5th House; Taurus – 4th House; Gemini – 3rd House; Cancer – 2nd House; Leo – 1st House; Virgo – 12th House; Libra – 11th House; Scorpio – 10th House; Sagittarius – 9th House; Capricorn – 8th House; Aquarius – 7th House; Pisces – 6th House.

● Your New Moon Affirmation ●

I'm magnificent!

New Moon Wishes and Intentions List

This is the time to be bold and confident about your ability to consciously create the life of your dreams. As you go about it, though, bear in mind this excellent advice from Gabby Bernstein in her book *Super Attractor*: 'True manifesting isn't even about getting what we think we want. It's about receiving what is of the highest good for all...'

_____

_____

_____

_____

_____

_____

_____

_____

_____

_____

_____

_____

Questions to Ask at This New Moon

Which of the following statements applies to you?

1. I'm nicely confident.
2. I'm over-confident.
3. I'm under-confident?

_____

_____

(If you answered 2 or 3): How would my life change if I were nicely confident?

_____

_____

_____

_____

Who in your life has 'just enough' confidence and you can speak to for advice?

_____

_____

_____

_____

AUGUST Week 32

2 MONDAY ♉♊ ◐

3 TUESDAY ♊ ◐

4 WEDNESDAY ♊♋ ◑

5 THURSDAY ♋ ●

FRIDAY 6

SATURDAY 7

SUNDAY 8

New Moon
London   14:50
Sydney   23:50
Los Angeles   06:50
New York   09:50

THIS WEEK

There's some heavy-duty Saturn action this week, so make sure
you're being grown-up. Issues that come up now are here to
teach you important lessons that you missed out on earlier.

AUGUST WEEK 33

....

9 MONDAY   ♌ ♍ 🌑

....

10 TUESDAY   ♍ 🌑

....

11 WEDNESDAY   ♍ ♎ 🌒

....

12 THURSDAY   ♎ 🌒

....

☽ ♎︎   FRIDAY 13

☽ ♎︎ ♏︎   SATURDAY 14

☽ ♏︎   SUNDAY 15

What are you grateful for right now?

THIS WEEK

*A week that's good for romance, but it could also bring
out someone's deceptive nature, so if you're entangled
with someone who isn't on the level, beware.*

Blue Full Moon in Aquarius

The key energies of this Moon are:
Opportunity • You Only Live Once • Faith • Rarity

Place	Date	Time	Degrees
London	22 August	13:01	29:37
Sydney	22 August	22:01	29:37
Los Angeles	22 August	05:01	29:37
New York	22 August	08:01	29:37

This month's Full Moon takes place in Aquarius, as did the last. The reason is that there are 30 degrees in each sign: the last Full Moon in Aquarius took place in the very early degrees of Aquarius (at 01 degree), whereas this month's takes place at the very end of the sign (29 degrees).

There are various definitions of a Blue Moon and none of them are astrological; rather, they are astronomical. In this case, the Full Moon is 'Blue' because it's the third Full Moon in a season (here, summer) with four Full Moons.

If there's something you're trying to achieve, or more specifically, trying to release, try again now. Do you have resistance to something in your life, and is it blocking you from achieving your goals? This Full Moon gives you more or less a second chance to let it go and do some forgiveness work. There's nearly always someone to forgive – whether it's yourself or someone else – so re-read the Formula for Forgiveness and Karma Release (*see page 61*). Also consider the symbolism of the Leo/Aquarius axis, which this Full Moon straddles. The Leo energy is showy and bold, while the Aquarius energy is detached and cool. Somewhere in all our lives, we *really* need to find a balance between these energies.

What this Lunation Means for You

To discover where the energy of this Full Moon is for you, find your Star sign or Rising sign here, see which House is involved, and then read the Full Moon through the Houses guide (*see pages 14–17*): Aries – 11th House; Taurus – 10th House; Gemini – 9th House; Cancer – 8th House; Leo – 7th House; Virgo – 6th House; Libra – 5th House; Scorpio – 4th House; Sagittarius – 3rd House; Capricorn – 2nd House; Aquarius – 1st House; Pisces – 12th House.

After the Full Moon

The first alignment after this Full Moon is a harmonious one between Venus, the planet of love and abundance, and Saturn, the planet of longevity. Make a list of any new commitments to do with love or abundance and how you feel you can achieve them. Most importantly, consider what you need to release from your life to make this happen. Write that down too, and then burn it right after you burn your Full Moon forgiveness list at your Full Moon ceremony.

Full Moon Forgiveness List

With two Full Moons in the same sign for two consecutive months, it's as if the Universe *knows* you're having problems divesting yourself of something troubling. So what is it? The House information this month could give you some insight. Whatever it is, feel who or what in this situation needs forgiving, and then do it!

_____

_____

_____

_____

_____

_____

_____

_____

_____

_____

_____

_____

_____

✳ Questions to Ask at This Full Moon

How can I detach from my biggest fear or worry?

_____

_____

_____

_____

What am I refusing to relinquish?

_____

_____

_____

_____

Where am I being too proud?

_____

_____

_____

_____

_____

AUGUST WEEK 34

16 MONDAY ♏ ♐ ☽

17 TUESDAY ♐ ☽

18 WEDNESDAY ♐ ♑ ☽

19 THURSDAY ♑ ☽

○ ♑ ♒   FRIDAY 20

○ ♒   SATURDAY 21

○ ♒ ♓   SUNDAY 22

Blue Full Moon
London   13:01
Sydney   22:01
Los Angeles   05:01
New York   08:01

THIS WEEK

There's a Blue Moon this week – a Full Moon in the sign
of Aquarius. Release, release, release. The cool Aquarian
energies will make this easier than usual to do.

AUGUST WEEK 35

....

23 MONDAY   ♓○

....

24 TUESDAY   ♓♈○

....

25 WEDNESDAY   ♈○

....

26 THURSDAY   ♈☽

....

◐♈♉

FRIDAY 27

◐♉

SATURDAY 28

◐♉♊

SUNDAY 29

THIS WEEK

*We're now in the waning cycle of the Moon, but it's
still a good time to make an agreement that will stick
– perhaps the Full Moon brought you clarity?*

September

A t the very least, this is a month to get organized! We get the New Moon in Virgo, the sign of organization, and the Full Moon in Pisces, the sign that can be a tad messy. All in all, it's a great time to start with new and tidier habits and to release messy tendencies.

If you start this month feeling a tad confused, stick with it. By the first week of September, clarity could well have come, thanks to a connection between Mercury and Saturn. It feels as if we're now getting down to the business end of the year, so if there are things you'd still like to accomplish between now and December, this is a great month to make a list. List-making really is a super-powerful technique for making life changes. Somehow, the very act of expressing an idea on paper seems to kick-start the process of making it real.

Also, in the second half of September, Venus, the planet of love and abundance, is slightly in the wars – but it all ends well. Based on the 'as above, so below' theory on which astrology is founded, this could see some of us going through distinct ups and downs to do with matters of the heart or the bank balance. There could be dramas, followed by happier days; followed by the feeling that someone or something is in your way or trying its utmost to make you miserable; followed by excitement, changes, dreams coming true and finally, almost too much of a good thing.

M	T	W	T	F	S	S
		1	2	3	4	5
6	7 ●	8	9	10	11	12
13 ◑	14	15	16	17	18	19
20 ○	21	22	23	24	25	26
27	28	29 ◐	30			

~ Things to do this month ~

1. Get organized.
2. Admit where you're muddled.
3. Believe in love.

AUG/SEPT WEEK 36

. . . .

30 MONDAY   ♊ ◑

What are you grateful for right now?
. . . .

31 TUESDAY   ♊ ◑

. . . .

1 WEDNESDAY   ♊♋ ◑

. . . .

2 THURSDAY   ♋ ◑

. . . .

● ♋♌   Friday 3

● ♌   Saturday 4

● ♌♍   Sunday 5

This Week

This Third Quarter Moon week is great for anyone who does what could be considered a 'spooky' activity, such as yoga, Tai Chi or Chi Gung. A Mars/Neptune opposition will take your practice further.

New Moon in Virgo

The key energies of this Moon are:
Organization • Discernment • Dreaminess • Insight

Place	Date	Time	Degrees
London	7 September	01:51	14:38
Sydney	7 September	10:51	14:38
Los Angeles	6 September	17:51	14:38
New York	6 September	20:51	14:38

There's a strong push me/pull you energy in this New Moon. On the one hand, it's taking place in arguably the most organized sign of the zodiac, Virgo. This is the sign that counts beans, crosses t's and dots i's. Remember, we all have this energy in our chart somewhere: see 'What this lunation means for you' to find out where in your chart it is and where you can get organized.

But on the other hand, this New Moon is also triggering a rather powerful Mars/Neptune opposition. Action planet Mars is the trigger, whereas Neptune is the planet of dreams and doziness. So it's a time to get organized, but in a way that inspires you. You could perhaps organize your work desk, so you feel more inspired to be professionally productive.

The New Moon is also making a harmonious aspect to the planet of change and chaos, Uranus. This could mean that if you take time to do something like declutter your home, it'll all work in your favour very quickly. If getting your life in order was one of your aims as you came into 2021, now is the time to check in with how you're doing. If you aren't on course, make a correction.

☧ A Virgo Ritual

Treat yourself to a bunch of long-stemmed flowers and then place them in a circle around you on the floor. Sit and breathe deeply and call in Virgo's grounding energies. Recite the following: 'I'm grounded to the Earth and I draw energy up from her. I call on the energy of Virgo to keep me earthed. And so it is!' You can gather up the flowers and put them in a vase afterwards.

☧ What This Lunation Means for You

To discover where the energy of this New Moon is for you, find your Star sign or Rising sign here, see which House is involved, and then read the New Moon through the Houses guide (*see pages 10–14*): Aries – 6th House; Taurus – 5th House; Gemini – 4th House; Cancer – 3rd House; Leo – 2nd House; Virgo – 1st House; Libra – 12th House; Scorpio – 11th House; Sagittarius – 10th House; Capricorn – 9th House; Aquarius – 8th House; Pisces – 7th House.

● Your New Moon Affirmation ●

Exciting changes are coming my way.

New Moon Wishes and Intentions List

Virgo is one of the two signs (Gemini is the other) that are strongly associated with the planet of writing and reading, Mercury. So even if you've been lazy about making your New Moon wishes lately, this is the month to get that pen back in your hand.

_____

_____

_____

_____

_____

_____

_____

_____

_____

_____

_____

_____

Questions to Ask at This New Moon

Can I improve my health by eliminating unnecessary stress? What can I try?

_____

_____

_____

_____

What's the #1 stumbling block to my being organized, and what can I do about it?

_____

_____

_____

_____

Am I being reliable to the people who rely on me? If not, what can I do about it?

_____

_____

_____

_____

SEPTEMBER WEEK 37

. . . .

6 MONDAY   ♍

New Moon
Los Angeles   17:51
New York   20:51

. . . .

7 TUESDAY   ♍ ●

New Moon
London   01:51
Sydney   10:51

. . . .

8 WEDNESDAY   ♍♎

. . . .

9 THURSDAY   ♎ ◑

. . . .

◗ ♎ ♏

FRIDAY 10

◗ ♏

SATURDAY 11

◗ ♏ ♐

SUNDAY 12

THIS WEEK

*It's New Moon week. Be sure to take the time to write
out your New Moon wishes and intentions. By now, I
hope you know how powerful an exercise this is!*

SEPTEMBER WEEK 38

13 MONDAY

What are you grateful for right now?

14 TUESDAY

15 WEDNESDAY

16 THURSDAY

○ ♒   Friday 17

○ ♒ ♓   Saturday 18

○ ♓   Sunday 19

This Week

*A tricky Venus/Saturn link means you could feel as if there's
not enough love to go around. This feeling, too, shall pass!
Interrupt any anxiety you feel about love or abundance
issues with gratitude for the good in your life.*

Full Moon in Pisces

The key energies of this Moon are:
Soulfulness • Seduction • Deception • Disappointment

Place	Date	Time	Degrees
London	21 September	00:54	28:13
Sydney	21 September	09:54	28:13
Los Angeles	20 September	16:54	28:13
New York	20 September	19:54	28:13

This is a powerful time of year. We have what's known in astro-speak as a Grand Trine (a massive triangle) made by two planets and a point: Mars, Pluto and the North Node. That's a good thing because a Grand Trine means that the energy flows easily. Now, under the Full Moon, it can be interpreted as the drive to release resistance, which allows us to get back on our soul path.

So, are you ready for this? Every Full Moon offers us a chance to release and let go. This one will make releasing for our highest good easier and better. Also know that this Full Moon triggers Neptune, the modern Pisces planet. This essentially means there's more Piscean/Neptune energy around than at your average Full Moon in Pisces. This energy is mysterious and spiritual; tap into it on the night of the Full Moon with a mystical ceremony (*see below*).

Pisces is the last sign of the zodiac, so this last Full Moon marks the end of a period in our lives. Think about what you've released in the past 12 months, and how your connection to the Divine has changed.

Soon after the Full Moon we get a Mercury/Pluto clash, so this Full Moon may seem to be winding you up.

✳ What This Lunation Means for You

To discover where the energy of this Full Moon is for you, find your Star sign or Rising sign here, see which House is involved, and then read the Full Moon through the Houses guide (*see pages 14–17*): Aries – 12th House; Taurus – 11th House; Gemini – 10th House; Cancer – 9th House; Leo – 8th House; Virgo – 7th House; Libra – 6th House; Scorpio – 5th House; Sagittarius – 4th House; Capricorn – 3rd House; Aquarius – 2nd House; Pisces – 1st House.

✳ A Mystical Full Moon Ceremony

As we move through this last Full Moon for this cycle, it's time to clear away the past. As well as writing your Full Moon forgiveness list, you could cleanse yourself and your space by burning sage (just make sure it's reliably sourced). Sage is an effective energy cleaner, and research has shown that burning sage removes 94 per cent of bacteria in the air. To cleanse yourself, light a sage stick and waft the smoke towards you with your hands or a feather, twirling around as you do so.

Full Moon Forgiveness List

So here we go – this one's a biggie! Firstly, Pisces is the sign of compassion, and there's not a lot that's more compassionate than forgiving someone or yourself for things done or not done. Secondly, this is the last Full Moon of this cycle – so forgive *big*. Pour out your heart.

Questions to Ask at This Full Moon

What does not forgiving [name of person] do for me?

_____

_____

_____

_____

How could I be kinder to myself and others?

_____

_____

_____

_____

Can I draw a line in the sand and move on this month?

_____

_____

_____

_____

_____

SEPTEMBER WEEK 39

· ·

20 MONDAY

♓ ○

Full Moon
Los Angeles   16:54
New York   19:54

· ·

21 TUESDAY

♓ ♈ ○

Full Moon
London   00:54
Sydney   09:54

· ·

22 WEDNESDAY

♈ ○

Autumn Equinox/Mabon (northern hemisphere) and
Spring Equinox/Ostara (southern hemisphere)

· ·

23 THURSDAY

♈ ♉ ○

· ·

◐ ♉   FRIDAY 24

◐ ♉   SATURDAY 25

◐ ♉♊   SUNDAY 26

THIS WEEK

*Note that this is the final week before the new Mercury retrograde
cycle starts, so be prepared. Not sure what to do? Grab a copy of my*
Mercury Retrograde Book *at mercuryretrogradebook.com.*

October

When you look at the ephemeris (the book of planetary positions) for this month, you'll see several little squares which, in astrology, represent planetary clashes. They also represent an itch that needs to be scratched; in other words, when there are squares in the air (which is when planets are at a 90-degree angle to each other) you'll often get mini crises that need to be attended to.

Something awkward will happen which you can't ignore and will require action. The five October 'squares' suggest we're going into a month where we might get a few dramas. There will be discomforts that prod us into taking action – with squares, life can be so uncomfortable that the effort of doing nothing at all is more stressful than biting the bullet and taking difficult action.

On top of the squares themselves is the astro-fact that these squares are triggering three major so-called 'outer' planets: Saturn, Neptune and Pluto. This makes the whole picture even more intense. These planets are all slower-moving than others, so when they do make connections, it's rather more momentous.

This month we get faster-moving planets – the Sun, Mercury and Mars – all clashing and colliding. The hot dates are 1, 17, 22, 27 and 30 October. But essentially, when you have these kinds of energies spread out through the month like this, it makes *all* of it hot – not least because we'll also feel all this in the lead-up, as well as on the day itself. That said, for sure, the second half of the month is even hotter.

M	T	W	T	F	S	S
				1	2	3
4	5	6 ●	7	8	9	10
11	12	13 ◐	14	15	16	17
18	19	20 ○	21	22	23	24
25	26	27	28 ◑	29	30	31

~ Things to do this month ~

1. Scratch a metaphorical itch.
2. Don't just sit there...
3. Do something!

SEPTEMBER WEEK 40

. . . .

27 MONDAY ♊︎◐

Mercury goes retrograde (until 18 October).
. . . .

28 TUESDAY ♊︎♋︎◐

. . . .

29 WEDNESDAY ♋︎◐

What are you grateful for right now?
. . . .

30 THURSDAY ♋︎◐

. . . .

☽♋♌ FRIDAY 1

☽♌ SATURDAY 2

☽♌♍ SUNDAY 3

THIS WEEK

*There's a lot of love in the air now as loving Venus connects
with dreamy Neptune, excessive Jupiter and passionate
Pluto, in that order. Expect dreamy, powerful love, but avoid
smothering your beloved with too much adoration.*

New Moon in Libra

The key energies of this Moon are:
Love • Libido • Drive • Ebullience

Place	Date	Time	Degrees
London	6 October	12:05	13:24
Sydney	6 October	22:05	13:24
Los Angeles	6 October	04:05	13:24
New York	6 October	07:05	13:24

One thing to know straight away is that this New Moon is *the* New Moon of the year in which to think about and work on your relationships (Libra being the sign of those). So think about where you are with the people who matter most to you, and what you can do between now and the end of the year to show them how much you care. As well, consider your professional relationships: do they need shoring up in the run-up to the holidays?

The good news is that this New Moon is making a rather wide link to the planet of plenty, Jupiter. In other words, it's going to be a little easier than usual to parlay this lunation into good relations with someone who matters to you. Jupiter has a lucky edge to it: when it's involved, good fortune follows. When Jupiter is being triggered, as it is this week, life tends to be easier rather than challenging.

Having this year's New Moon in the relationship sign of Libra connecting with Jupiter doesn't mean we're all going to have 100 per cent smooth relationships over the coming year, but it's definitely a fairly auspicious omen. Note that Mars is right near the lunation, too, so there's going to be a lot of fire in the air. In the right relationships, that can translate as good old-fashioned lust. Tune in, if you want to.

This New Moon, tune in to the three Goddesses of love: Aphrodite (Greek), Venus (Roman) and Lakshmi (Hindu). All three Goddesses attract abundance – material, emotional and spiritual.

Last but not least, note that Mercury is retrograde under this New Moon, so for some, it's an amazing chance for a romantic or platonic relationship restart.

What This Lunation Means for You

To discover where the energy of this New Moon is for you, find your Star sign or Rising sign here, see which House is involved, and then read the New Moon through the Houses guide (*see pages 10–14*): Aries – 7th House; Taurus – 6th House; Gemini – 5th House; Cancer – 4th House; Leo – 3rd House; Virgo – 2nd House; Libra – 1st House; Scorpio – 12th House; Sagittarius – 11th House; Capricorn – 10th House; Aquarius – 9th House; Pisces – 8th House.

● Your New Moon Affirmation ●

All my relationships are getting better and better.

New Moon Wishes and Intentions List

We all need good relationships, right? We're not *only* talking about romantic relationships here – we need good relationships with family and friends, colleagues and clients too. This is the month to include wishes for this in your New Moon ceremony. Remember to listen to the creative visualization meditation audio (moonmessages.com/diary2021) first.

_____

_____

_____

_____

_____

_____

_____

_____

_____

_____

_____

_____

✵ Questions to Ask at This New Moon

Am I being my best self in my relationships? If not, how can I work on that?

_____

_____

_____

_____

Am I giving and getting in equal measure in my relationships?

_____

_____

_____

_____

What would 'the best outcome' look like in my most important relationships?

_____

_____

_____

_____

OCTOBER   WEEK 41

....

4 MONDAY   ♍ ●

....

5 TUESDAY   ♍♎ ●

....

6 WEDNESDAY   ♎ ●

New Moon
London   12:05
Sydney   22:05
Los Angeles   04:05
New York   07:05

....

7 THURSDAY   ♎♏ ●

....

●︎ ♏︎

FRIDAY 8

●︎ ♏︎ ♐︎

SATURDAY 9

◐︎ ♐︎

SUNDAY 10

THIS WEEK

*The New Moon in partnership-loving Libra this week is powered
by Mars. Expect some warmth and even fire in your most important
one-to-one relationships – whether personal or professional.*

OCTOBER Week 42

....

11 MONDAY ♐♑ 🌗

....

12 TUESDAY ♑ 🌗

....

13 WEDNESDAY ♑♒ 🌗

What are you grateful for right now?
....

14 THURSDAY ♒ 🌗

....

◯♒   FRIDAY 15

◯♒♓   SATURDAY 16

◯♓   SUNDAY 17

THIS WEEK

This week sees a lovely Venus/Saturn link, hot on the heels of the Venus-loving Libra New Moon. Good relationships can go from strength to strength now. Make the effort and expect the best.

Full Moon in Aries

The key energies of this Moon are:
Rebirth • Realities • Struggles • Forgiveness

Place	Date	Time	Degrees
London	20 October	15:56	27:26
Sydney	21 October	01:56	27:26
Los Angeles	20 October	07:56	27:26
New York	20 October	10:56	27:26

The first thing to note about this Full Moon is that it's the first one in the new lunar cycle. The previous Full Moon was in Pisces, the last of the 12 signs of the zodiac, and Aries is the first sign. So if you want to see what happens in your life when you work with the Full Moon every month, now's the time to commit.

While working with the New Moon is fun and amazing, it's working with the Full Moon and releasing resistance through forgiveness and surrender that truly allows us to consciously create our lives. Why? Because in doing that release work, we become more energetically clear and when that happens, it's much easier for us to send out our dreams to the Universe.

Think of yourself like a radio. When you're energetically clear, you're tuned in to the right station on the right frequency, and broadcasting your intentions clearly. In other words, what we feel is what we put out to the Universe, and what we put out is what comes back to us. So release anger and upset and resentment at the Full Moon and you'll feel good. And when you feel good, you manifest/attract/create good things, consciously or not.

These are all things to think about at this Full Moon, which looks like being fiery and perhaps extra emotional.

⚹ What This Lunation Means for You

To discover where the energy of this Full Moon is for you, find your Star sign or Rising sign here, see which House is involved, and then read the Full Moon through the Houses guide (*see pages 14–17*): Aries – 1st House; Taurus – 12th House; Gemini – 11th House; Cancer – 10th House; Leo – 9th House; Virgo – 8th House; Libra – 7th House; Scorpio – 6th House; Sagittarius – 5th House; Capricorn – 4th House; Aquarius – 3rd House; Pisces – 2nd House.

⚹ Commit to Working with the Full Moon

To honour the first of the Full Moons in the new 12-month cycle, make a pledge to work with *all* the Full Moons coming your way for the next 12 months.

I pledge to work with the coming 12 Full Moons – forgiving, surrendering, and releasing resistance to my dreams.

Signed ....

Full Moon Forgiveness List

When you forgive, a magical, alchemical thing happens: you release karma and the Moon's frequency allows you to feel better about yourself and move on. So dig deep and forgive whomever you can, including yourself. Perform a ceremony using essential oils, a red candle and sacred music. Make a list of the people you're forgiving, and then burn it.

_____

_____

_____

_____

_____

_____

_____

_____

_____

_____

_____

_____

Questions to Ask at This Full Moon

Do I understand that forgiveness doesn't make what happened okay? Who is going to feel better, lighter and happier if I forgive [name of person]. Them or me?

_____

_____

_____

Do I understand that holding on to anger only harms me? (Express your thoughts about why holding on to anger is a bad thing.)

_____

_____

_____

Am I willing to forgive the people who've hurt me the most? If not, why not?

_____

_____

_____

_____

OCTOBER WEEK 43

....

18 MONDAY   ♓♈○

Mercury retrograde ends.
....

19 TUESDAY   ♈○

....

20 WEDNESDAY   ♈♉○

Full Moon
London   15:56
Los Angeles   07:56
New York   10:56

....

21 THURSDAY   ♉○

Full Moon
Sydney   01:56

....

○ ♉   FRIDAY 22

○ ♉♊   SATURDAY 23

○ ♊   SUNDAY 24

THIS WEEK

*It's a big week as Mercury retrograde ends in the sign of Libra
and the Full Moon takes place in the sign of Aries, opposite
Libra. Wherever these signs are in your chart is a hotspot!*

OCTOBER WEEK 44

25 MONDAY   ♊ ♋ ◐

26 TUESDAY   ♋ ◐

27 WEDNESDAY   ♋ ◐

28 THURSDAY   ♋ ♌ ◑

What are you grateful for right now?

◗ ♌   FRIDAY 29

◗ ♌♍   SATURDAY 30

◗ ♍   SUNDAY 31

Festivals of Samhain (northern hemisphere)
and Beltane (southern hemisphere)

THIS WEEK

This is an interesting time for love and abundance, in particular.
There could be confusion early on this week, but it looks like working
out fine. Watch out if you find yourself lecturing someone. Be nice!

November

Welcome to an eclipse month. In other words, hang on, because it's going to be a ride! This is a Full Moon eclipse in the sign of Taurus. More about what this means later, but know that when there's an eclipse about, life changes. This is particularly true if you have your Sun, Moon or Rising sign in Taurus, but it will affect everyone.

Think of an eclipse as when the Universe changes gears. Life really can change at an eclipse. And if your life really *needs* to change but you're resisting it, watch out. Sometimes an eclipse, especially a Full Moon eclipse, forces us to release our grip on something.

It's like the torrid relationship I once had with a hard-drinking but oh-so charming philanderer. I knew I had to leave, but as long as he lied his pretty lies, I chose to believe him, against my intuition... until an eclipse came along and ended it for me. Breaking up with that man was the hardest thing I've ever done, apart from giving birth. That's an eclipse for you: if you're off track, they will put you unceremoniously back on track. The closer to your chart they are, the more you'll feel it.

However, if you leave it to the eclipse to sort you out, the whole process becomes far more painful. So if you know there's something in your life you need to walk away from, leave behind, release, do it now.

The good news is that after the eclipse, we get a super-soothing Saturn/Chiron link, which will be healing. Plus the New Moon this month is a Super New Moon.

M	T	W	T	F	S	S
1	2	3	4 ●	5	6	7
8	9	10	11 ◐	12	13	14
15	16	17	18	19 ○	20	21
22	23	24	25	26	27 ◐	28
29	30					

~ Things to do this month ~

1. Let it go.
2. Move on.
3. Heal.

Super New Moon in Scorpio

The key energies of this Moon are:
Escape • Outrageousness • Sex • Awakenings

Place	Date	Time	Degrees
London	4 November	21:14	12:40
Sydney	5 November	08:14	12:40
Los Angeles	4 November	14:14	12:40
New York	4 November	17:14	12:40

Like they say on the radio, the hits just keep coming. This month, even before we go into the next eclipse season, we have the New Moon in deep, dark Scorpio, closely aligned with the outrageous maverick planet Uranus. In other words, the skies are electric around the November New Moon. If at the end of this year you feel like you're skidding towards the finishing line, that's why.

This will have been a very challenging year for many, thanks to all the jarring alignments I mentioned in the introduction to this diary. But we're nearly at the end of it. So all that remains is (a) being grateful for all the good in your life and (b) asking yourself if you've learned the lessons that this year has been trying to teach you.

If you're feeling stuck, this New Moon really does have your back. Being as close to Uranus as it is, it's like electric shock therapy that rips off the old – all of a sudden, and even a tad thoughtlessly. Sudden changes and turnarounds are possible now, so don't write off 2021 if it doesn't seem to be ending as you'd like it to. Instead, use the power surge of this lunation to make bold choices, decisions and intentions.

As you might know, manifesting is not just about wishing. It's also about taking follow-up action, so think about what you can do to make your dreams become real. With Uranus active now, ingenuity and individuality will be applauded.

Do you need to stop judging someone, maybe yourself. Print out a picture of someone you've judged and set it on your altar/a table. Light a pink candle and then visualize love coming from your heart chakra and enveloping them. Ask them for forgiveness.

ᛉ What This Lunation Means for You

To discover where the energy of this New Moon is for you, find your Star sign or Rising sign here, see which House is involved, and then read the New Moon through the Houses guide (*see pages 10–14*): Aries – 8th House; Taurus – 7th House; Gemini – 6th House; Cancer – 5th House; Leo – 4th House; Virgo – 3rd House; Libra – 2nd House; Scorpio – 1st House; Sagittarius – 12th House; Capricorn – 11th House; Aquarius – 10th House; Pisces – 9th House.

● Your New Moon Affirmation ●

I'm grateful for all the good in my life.

New Moon Wishes and Intentions List

A few ideas for you this month: wish for enlightenment; wish for something to turn around; wish to be liberated from something that's holding you back; wish to stop judging; wish to lose any inhibitions that hold you back in life. Wish like mad!

_____

_____

_____

_____

_____

_____

_____

_____

_____

_____

_____

_____

⚕ Questions to Ask at This New Moon

Where in my life do I need to break free? Am I going to do it?

_____

_____

_____

_____

What would I do if I cared less about what people think?

_____

_____

_____

_____

How can I improve my sex life?

_____

_____

_____

_____

NOVEMBER WEEK 45

1 MONDAY   ♍︎♎︎ 🌑

2 TUESDAY   ♎︎ 🌑

3 WEDNESDAY   ♎︎ 🌑

4 THURSDAY   ♎︎♏︎ 🌑

Super Full Moon
London   21:14
Los Angeles   14:14
New York   17:14

● ♏

FRIDAY 5

Super Full Moon
Sydney   08:14

● ♏ ♐

SATURDAY 6

● ♐

SUNDAY 7

THIS WEEK

*To turn your life around this New Moon week, be radical
and don't be afraid of a 180-degree pivot. Don't worry too
much about conforming. Dig deep into your feelings.*

NOVEMBER WEEK 46

....

8 MONDAY ♐♑ ◑

....

9 TUESDAY ♑ ◑

....

10 WEDNESDAY ♑♒ ◑

....

11 THURSDAY ♒ ◑

What are you grateful for right now?
....

◐ ♒︎ ♓︎   FRIDAY 12

◐ ♓︎   SATURDAY 13

◐ ♓︎ ♈︎   SUNDAY 14

THIS WEEK

There's a difficult Mars/Saturn clash now. Mars is the planet
that likes to push forwards, while Saturn is the Great Obstacle.
If you're banging your head against a brick wall, stop.

Full Moon Eclipse in Taurus

The key energies of this Moon are:
Change • Pardoning • Expressiveness • Possessiveness

Place	Date	Time	Degrees
London	19 November	08:57	27:14
Sydney	19 November	19:57	27:14
Los Angeles	19 November	00:57	27:14
New York	19 November	03:57	27:14

The Full Moon eclipse ushers in the start of the last eclipse season of 2021. Among other things, Taurus is strongly associated with creature comforts and the money that's needed to buy them. If you want a turnaround of the flow of cash into your life, now is the time to work on it.

The thing to remember is that money is energy and it responds to your expectations. If you value yourself (values are also Taurean), you'll attract more cash. It's that simple. People who are clear that they want money, and aren't afraid to seek it out, are far more likely to attract it than people who think that money is the root of all evil (the original Bible quote says that *the love* of money is the root of all evil, not money itself).

While I was writing this year's diary, someone said to me: 'Anyone who's a medium or psychic and doesn't have much cash... don't trust them!' Her point was that once you're in the flow of life, you're in the flow of abundance.

Remember, because money is energy, you'll attract it or repel it as you see fit. If you think all rich people are evil, then you're unlikely to become rich. If you think money can do amazing things, including great charitable works, you're far more likely to end up as a wealthy philanthropist.

⚸ What This Lunation Means for You

To discover where the energy of this Full Moon is for you, find your Star sign or Rising sign here, see which House is involved, and then read the Full Moon through the Houses guide (*see pages 14–17*): Aries – 2nd House; Taurus – 1st House; Gemini – 12th House; Cancer – 11th House; Leo – 10th House; Virgo – 9th House; Libra – 8th House; Scorpio – 7th House; Sagittarius – 6th House; Capricorn – 5th House; Aquarius – 4th House; Pisces – 3rd House.

⚸ How Do You Feel about Money?

The Full Moon eclipse in Taurus is an ideal time to release any negativity you feel around money. Think back to your childhood and what your parents taught you about money. Did they treat it as a dirty subject, never to be discussed, or did they teach you about its value? Make a note and use it to analyse your current financial situation. If you're a parent, teach your children that generosity creates more abundance and that there's more than enough to go around.

Full Moon Forgiveness List

Use this Full Moon to release any negative ideas you have about money and forgive anyone who you believe may have given you those negative ideas. They were probably just preaching what they'd been taught, but you can break the cycle here and now, if you choose to. And of course, forgive anyone else you need to.

_____

_____

_____

_____

_____

_____

_____

_____

_____

_____

_____

⚺ Questions to Ask at This Full Moon

What are my beliefs around money? Do they need changing?

_____

_____

_____

_____

How's my love life? Could I send more love into the world?

_____

_____

_____

_____

List the top 3 things you're no longer going to waste your money on.

_____

_____

_____

_____

NOVEMBER WEEK 47

15 MONDAY ♈○

16 TUESDAY ♈○

17 WEDNESDAY ♈♉○

18 THURSDAY ♉○

○ ♉♊

FRIDAY 19

Full Moon eclipse
London   08:57
Sydney   19:57
Los Angeles 00:57
New York   03:57

○ ♊

SATURDAY 20

○ ♊

SUNDAY 21

THIS WEEK

*It's an eclipse week, so all bets are off. Try not to act
out. There's a big Mars/Uranus clash along with
the eclipse, so the energies are super-high.*

NOVEMBER WEEK 48

....

22 MONDAY   ♊ ♋ ○

....

23 TUESDAY   ♋ ○

....

24 WEDNESDAY   ♋ ♌ ○

....

25 THURSDAY   ♌ ○

....

....

◗ ♌   FRIDAY 26

....

 ♌ ♍   SATURDAY 27

What are you grateful for right now?
....

◑ ♍   SUNDAY 28

....

THIS WEEK

*The Sun and Mercury move into Sagittarius now, so expect
to be focused on wherever you have Sagittarius in your
chart. Find this out under 'What this lunation means for
you' under New Moon in Sagittarius (see page 237).*

December

It's quite the action-packed end to the year, proving once more that time is a man-made construct. We divide our lives into seconds, minutes, hours, days, weeks and so on. But although we seem to have cracked the concept of counting time as it passes, the truth is that we're on a planet spinning around a Sun, which is in a solar system, which is in a galaxy, and so on again.

One thing's for sure, though, 2021 is going out with a bang, piping some of the messages it's been shoving in our faces through the past 12 months. December brings a Super New Moon eclipse, for a start, and this time it's in the sign of Sagittarius. More of what that means coming up, but it certainly marks the first week of December as a time to start thinking about what you want for 2022 – which is coming at us fast.

Also this month, we have Venus the Goddess, the planet of love and abundance, caresses and pleasure, going into a rare retrograde cycle. Whereas Mercury retrogrades up to four times a year, Venus does so once every 18 months or so. This time she's doing it in Capricorn, which is an interesting combination pre-Christmas and could see retail sales hampered, or lots of Christmas gifts being returned after it.

It's also a time when we can reconsider who and what really matters to us, and plan to adjust our lives accordingly in 2022. This cycle lasts into next year.

As well, Saturn clashes with Uranus again. As the year ends, it's time to smash through your limitations.

M	T	W	T	F	S	S
		1	2	3	4 ●	5
6	7	8	9	10	11 ◑	12
13	14	15	16	17	18	19 ○
20	21	22	23	24	25	26
27 ◐	28	29	30	31		

~ Things to do this month ~

1. Start all over again (again!)

2. Work out what you really value.

3. Forgive and move on.

Super New Moon Eclipse
in Sagittarius

The key energies of this Moon are:
Communication • Fieriness • Tempers • Passion

Place	Date	Time	Degrees
London	4 December	07:43	12:22
Sydney	4 December	18:43	12:22
Los Angeles	3 December	23:43	12:22
New York	4 December	02:43	12:22

So here we are again: at the start of the end of the year, with a New Moon eclipse before us. This time around it's in Sagittarius, the cheery sign of idealism, justice and adventure. If you're planning to turn at least part of 2022 into a wild trip around the planet, this eclipse has your back, so set some intentions around that. Sagittarius is always striving – which is why its glyph, or symbol, is an arrow aiming for the heavens.

So what are you striving for? And how true is your aim? These are questions to think about now. If you want to educate yourself or widen your horizons in 2022, then this is the time to write that down and set it as a concrete intention. As I hope you've discovered over the course of this year, intentions are super-powerful – they really can change lives!

If 2021 has left you feeling a bit spent, the New Moon in Sagittarius is also a great time to get some fire in your belly about life. We have one more big clash before the year ends – Saturn/Uranus on Christmas Eve. So whatever actions you take under this eclipse, make sure that one of them is wishing for all the energy you need for a happy and healthy end to the year.

There's a lot of Neptune energy around, which could easily be just a case of 'too much eggnog'. But if you feel you need to be clearer now, follow your instincts and pledge to keep a clear head – all the tempting seasonal offers notwithstanding.

⚹ What This Lunation Means for You

To discover where the energy of this New Moon is for you, find your Star sign or Rising sign here, see which House is involved, and then read the New Moon through the Houses guide (*see pages 10–14*): Aries – 9th House; Taurus – 8th House; Gemini – 7th House; Cancer – 6th House; Leo – 5th House; Virgo – 4th House; Libra – 3rd House; Scorpio – 2nd House; Sagittarius – 1st House; Capricorn – 12th House; Aquarius – 11th House; Pisces – 10th House.

● Your New Moon Affirmation ●

My horizons are expanding every day.

New Moon Wishes and Intentions List

This New Moon eclipse is super-powerful for intentions and wishing. Moreover, it's taking place at the end of 2021. So if you only make one wish list this year, *make it this one*! Wish for what you want to attract in 2022.

_____

_____

_____

_____

_____

_____

_____

_____

_____

_____

_____

_____

_____

☿ Questions to Ask at This New Moon

What adventures do I want to have in the coming 12 months, starting this month?

_____

_____

_____

_____

Where in my life can I aim higher?

_____

_____

_____

_____

Where in my life do I lack clarity? What can I do about it?

_____

_____

_____

_____

Nov/Dec Week 49

- -

29 Monday   ♍♎ ◖

- -

30 Tuesday   ♎ ◖

- -

1 Wednesday   ♎♏ ◖

- -

2 Thursday   ♏ ●

- -

●︎ ♏︎➚♐︎   FRIDAY 3

Super New Moon eclipse
Los Angeles   23:43

●︎ ♐︎   SATURDAY 4

Super New Moon eclipse
London   07:43
Sydney   18:43
New York   02:43

◗ ♐︎♑︎   SUNDAY 5

THIS WEEK

*There's a New Moon eclipse this week, which means its
absolutely primo time for making wishes and setting intentions.
Whatever you do, don't wait for New Year. Just do it!*

DECEMBER WEEK 50

. . . .

6 MONDAY   ♑ ◗

. . . .

7 TUESDAY   ♑ ♒ ◗

. . . .

8 WEDNESDAY   ♒ ◗

. . . .

9 THURSDAY   ♒ ♓ ◗

. . . .

☽ ♓   FRIDAY 10

☽ ♓ ♈   SATURDAY 11

What are you grateful for right now?

☽ ♈   SUNDAY 12

THIS WEEK

There are some challenging energies around now, and because
Neptune's being triggered, we certainly all need to watch what
we imbibe. But overall, in the end, love will win the week.

Full Moon in Gemini

The key energies of this Moon are:
Endings • Beginnings • Authenticity • Values

Place	Date	Time	Degrees
London	19 December	04:35	27:28
Sydney	19 December	15:35	27:28
Los Angeles	18 December	20:35	27:28
New York	18 December	23:35	27:28

Think of this Full Moon as one of the end points of the year – because it is. The Full Moon in Gemini takes place in a beautiful aspect to the planet of plenty and good luck, Jupiter. The Full Moon in Gemini is also perfect for this time of the year. Gemini rules the mind and sits opposite Sagittarius, the most optimistic of all signs, so here we have the 'mind' highlighted at the end of the year, with optimistic energy swirling around it. In other words, now is the time to think back over 2021 and – again – be grateful.

Yes, I've asked you to be grateful many times in this diary. In fact, I suggest you practise gratitude on every single day this year. Gratitude moves mountains. 2021 has been quite intense, so there's been a lot of processing to do. Make sure you tap into the Full Moon now, with sincere gratitude for all the good that's come in the past 12 months. And then get ready to turn the page.

The end of the year is a man-made construct; however, it's also a very powerful one. Note that this Full Moon is taking place near the planet Jupiter, which is good news. The year-end can be very stressful, but with Jupiter active we should be able to laugh off any deadline dramas.

⚴ What This Lunation Means for You

To discover where the energy of this Full Moon is for you, find your Star sign or Rising sign here, see which House is involved, and then read the New Moon through the Houses guide (*see pages 14–17*): Aries – 3rd House; Taurus – 2nd House; Gemini – 1st House; Cancer – 12th House; Leo – 11th House; Virgo – 10th House; Libra – 9th House; Scorpio – 8th House; Sagittarius – 7th House; Capricorn – 6th House; Aquarius – 5th House; Pisces – 4th House.

⚴ A 'What I'm Releasing' List

If you're one of my regular readers you'll know that each year I encourage all who follow me to make a 'What I'm releasing' list. It comes before the 'What I'm drawing into my life in 20XX list'. It's important to get clear on where you are in life. Intention is everything. So, what do you intend to leave behind in 2021? Make your list and then... you've guessed it – burn it! As you do so, say,

I'm letting all these things go. I'm leaving them in the past. Thank you for everything, 2021. Now I'm moving on.

Full Moon Forgiveness List

Here it is: your last Full Moon forgiveness list of 2021. Because it's the end of the year, the best thing you can do is look back over the whole of the past 12 months and see where you *still* feel upset about something. Try again to forgive that situation. You can do it!

_____

_____

_____

_____

_____

_____

_____

_____

_____

_____

_____

Questions to Ask at This Full Moon

Where have I got into the habit of speaking or thinking negatively? Am I willing to stop that?

_____

_____

_____

_____

In which part of my life do I need to turn the page?

_____

_____

_____

_____

Which truth do I need to speak before the year ends?

_____

_____

_____

_____

December Week 51

....

13 Monday ♈︎🌕

....

14 Tuesday ♈︎♉︎🌕

....

15 Wednesday ♉︎🌕

....

16 Thursday ♉︎♊︎🌕

....

....

○ Ⅱ   Friday 17

....

○ Ⅱ   Saturday 18

Full Moon
Los Angeles   20:35
New York   23:35

....

○ Ⅱ ♋   Sunday 19

Full Moon
London   04:35
Sydney   15:35

Venus goes retrograde (until 29 January 2022).
....

This Week

*If you don't want to get caught up in the whole Venus
retrograde/taking-presents-back-to the-shops-after-Christmas
thing, buy your gifts now, before Venus retrograde begins.*

DECEMBER WEEK 52

....

20 MONDAY   ♋ ◯

....

21 TUESDAY   ♋♌ ◯

Winter Solstice/Yule (northern hemisphere) and
Summer Solstice/Litha (southern. hemisphere)
....

22 WEDNESDAY   ♌ ◯

....

23 THURSDAY   ♌ ◯

....

◒ ♌︎♍︎　　　　　　FRIDAY 24

◒ ♍︎　　　　　　SATURDAY 25

◓ ♍︎♎︎　　　　　　SUNDAY 26

THIS WEEK

On the one hand, there will be plenty of reasons to be cheerful this week. On the other, Saturn clashing with Uranus brings a last-minute, possibly uncomfortable, chance to wake up to yourself in 2021.

DECEMBER WEEK 53

....

27 MONDAY ♎︎ ◑

What are you grateful for right now?
....

28 TUESDAY ♎︎ ♏︎ ◑

....

29 WEDNESDAY ♏︎ ◑

....

30 THURSDAY ♏︎ ♐︎ ◑

....

WEEK 53 DEC/JAN 2022

FRIDAY **31**

♐

SATURDAY **1**

♐♑

SUNDAY **2**

♑

New Moon
London   18:33
Los Angeles   10:33
New York   13:33

THIS WEEK

If you haven't made your New Year's resolutions yet, a wonderful Mars/
Saturn alignment, which we'll feel on 29 December, is perfect for sitting
down and making your list. There is power in those words you write.

JANUARY

M	T	W	T	F	S	S
					1	2
3	4	5	6	7	8	9
10	11	12	13	14	15	16
17	18	19	20	21	22	23
24	25	26	27	28	29	30
31						

FEBRUARY

M	T	W	T	F	S	S
	1	2	3	4	5	6
7	8	9	10	11	12	13
14	15	16	17	18	19	20
21	22	23	24	25	26	27
28						

MARCH

M	T	W	T	F	S	S
	1	2	3	4	5	6
7	8	9	10	11	12	13
14	15	16	17	18	19	20
21	22	23	24	25	26	27
28	29	30	31			

APRIL

M	T	W	T	F	S	S
				1	2	3
4	5	6	7	8	9	10
11	12	13	14	15	16	17
18	19	20	21	22	23	24
25	26	27	28	29	30	

MAY

M	T	W	T	F	S	S
						1
2	3	4	5	6	7	8
9	10	11	12	13	14	15
16	17	18	19	20	21	22
23	24	25	26	27	28	29
30	31					

JUNE

M	T	W	T	F	S	S
		1	2	3	4	5
6	7	8	9	10	11	12
13	14	15	16	17	18	19
20	21	22	23	24	25	26
27	28	29	30			

JULY

M	T	W	T	F	S	S
				1	2	3
4	5	6	7	8	9	10
11	12	13	14	15	16	17
18	19	20	21	22	23	24
25	26	27	28	29	30	31

AUGUST

M	T	W	T	F	S	S
1	2	3	4	5	6	7
8	9	10	11	12	13	14
15	16	17	18	19	20	21
22	23	24	25	26	27	28
29	30	31				

SEPTEMBER

M	T	W	T	F	S	S
			1	2	3	4
5	6	7	8	9	10	11
12	13	14	15	16	17	18
19	20	21	22	23	24	25
26	27	28	29	30		

OCTOBER

M	T	W	T	F	S	S
					1	2
3	4	5	6	7	8	9
10	11	12	13	14	15	16
17	18	19	20	21	22	23
24	25	26	27	28	29	30
31						

NOVEMBER

M	T	W	T	F	S	S
	1	2	3	4	5	6
7	8	9	10	11	12	13
14	15	16	17	18	19	20
21	22	23	24	25	26	27
28	29	30				

DECEMBER

M	T	W	T	F	S	S
			1	2	3	4
5	6	7	8	9	10	11
12	13	14	15	16	17	18
19	20	21	22	23	24	25
26	27	28	29	30	31	

Notes

Notes

ABOUT THE AUTHOR

George Fetting

Yasmin Boland was born in Germany and grew up in Hobart, Tasmania. After university, she worked as a newspaper journalist which led her from Tasmania to 'mainland' Australia and eventually to London, where she worked as a journalist and radio and TV producer. In the 1990s, Yasmin learned how to meditate which completely changed her life. It also opened her up to astrology, which started as a hobby but eventually became her full-time job.

Yasmin is now one of the most widely read astrology writers on the planet. She loves all astrology but has a special interest in the Moon, and specifically in New and Full Moons. At her website yasminboland.com you can read her Daily Moon Message, along with her weekly, monthly and annual horoscopes. Yasmin is the bestselling author of *Moonology*, *Moonology Oracle Cards*, *Astrology Made Easy* and *The Mercury Retrograde Book*.

 yasminbolandsmoonology

 @yasminboland

 @moonologydotcom

yasminboland.com
moonology.com

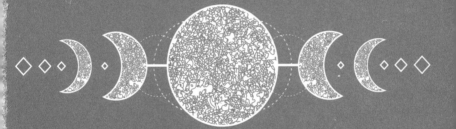

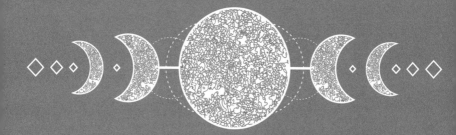